University of London
Institute of Commonwealth Studies

COMMONWEALTH PAPERS

*General Editor*
Professor W. H. Morris-Jones

16
Party and Locality in
Northern Uganda, 1945-1962

# COMMONWEALTH PAPERS

# Party and Locality in Northern Uganda, 1945-1962

*by*
CHERRY GERTZEL
*Professor of Political Science*
*University of Zambia*

UNIVERSITY OF LONDON
Published for the
Institute of Commonwealth Studies
THE ATHLONE PRESS
1974

*Published by*
THE ATHLONE PRESS
UNIVERSITY OF LONDON
*at* 4 *Gower Street, London* WC1

*Distributed by Tiptree Book Services Ltd*
*Tiptree, Essex*

*U.S.A. and Canada*
*Humanities Press Inc*
*New York*

ISBN 0 485 17616 5

*Printed in Great Britain by*
WESTERN PRINTING SERVICES LTD
BRISTOL

# PREFACE

This essay considers political developments in the two Northern Uganda districts of Acholi and Lango between 1945 and 1962. It is concerned primarily with the growth of political parties in these rural areas and the popular response at district level to the men who sought to develop those parties as a base from which to challenge the colonial government. Thus it seeks to add to our knowledge of African nationalism.

For a long time the study of African politics was characterized by a preoccupation with the national *macropolitical* level and the development of national institutions. This was largely true of most studies of political parties, which to a considerable extent ignored party leadership, recruitment, and ideas at the local level. More recently however there has been an increasing awareness of the importance of the political process at the local level for an understanding of the political process as a whole.[1] This emphasis upon micropolitics has led, among other developments, to a fresh enquiry into the growth of African nationalism and of political parties, with a change of focus from the political elite at the national level to the 'ordinary Africans' from whom the leaders had to obtain support.[2]

Such an emphasis on the local level is of great importance for any understanding of Uganda politics, which in the pre-independence period was dominated by the locality rather than the centre. There are some excellent studies of pre-independence politics, but these emphasized the national level, for a period when politics was largely decentralized and essentially *rural*-based. The district as a level of political activity was thus neglected. There are of course notable exceptions, particularly Southall's *Alur Society*,[3] Fallers' *Bantu Bureaucracy*,[4] and more recently Colin Leys' *Politicians and Policies*.[5] Generally, however, the district level received little attention until recently. Moreover, the emphasis was upon Buganda.[6] The reasons for that emphasis lay, of course, in the dominant position of that kingdom in Uganda, and the extent to which Ganda politics dictated national developments in the 1950s. The result was nevertheless that our knowledge of the growth of nationalism and of political parties at the grass roots level was very uneven. While a great deal is known about the reactions of the ordinary Ganda to the events of the fifties, much less is known about the role of the rural masses in other parts of the country in the same period. This essay attempts to redress the balance.

This is important because it was the overwhelming response of those rural masses outside Buganda to the appeal of the political parties in the 1961 and 1962 national elections that provided the non-Ganda leadership with sufficient bargaining strength to persuade Buganda to negotiate a settlement with them. Colin Leys has argued that the Uganda government's economic dependence on the mass of peasants as farmers underlay and reinforced its political dependence upon them as voters during the immediate post-independence period. The political dependence was crucial. It is important therefore to consider the growth of the national movement from the perspective of the rural voter and this requires us to examine the nationalist phenomenon at the local and rural as well as at the national level.

Anyone who lived in Kampala in the early 1960s could not moreover fail to be aware of the constant movement of party leaders between district and centre or of the frequency with which men from the districts visited the capital. Everything suggested a considerable interchange of influence between the two levels, a situation graphically illustrated by the crisis within both major parties, the Uganda People's Congress and the Democratic Party, at the time of the election of a Uganda President in 1963. At that time district leaders descended upon Kampala to press their views; behind the public debate in parliament and the private debate in the parliamentary groups of the parties there was a good deal of negotiation between the national leadership and local representatives.

The influence of the district on national politics was further suggested by the extent to which the government in the early years after independence coopted local elements in order to stabilize political rule. The alliance of the UPC with the Ganda movement Kabaka Yekka and the election of the Kabaka as President in 1963 were perhaps the most obvious, but there were numerous other indications of cooption, not only of Buganda but of other localities. District leaders figured prominently, for example, in the membership of the Regional Services Commission set up in 1962 to deal with appointments to the local government civil service.

Political developments in Uganda after 1962 furthermore saw 'the North' emerge as an increasingly significant factor in a country hitherto dominated by Buganda. Allegations of 'Northern dominance' had by 1966 replaced earlier charges against Buganda; the contest between the former Prime Minister, Milton Obote, and the former President, Kabaka Mutesa II, which reached its climax in 1966, was seen by many as a conflict between 'North' and 'South'. It is my own view that the lines of conflict were in fact by no means so sharply cut between the two regions. Nevertheless one must ask what was the basis of the increased prominence of the Northern districts. Part of it was clearly the former Prime Minister's UPC support in those districts, yet we know little about how it was built up. This essay seeks to increase our knowledge of a part of the Northern scene in the years before independence, when the foundations of that support were laid. In doing so it is hoped that something more will be added to our understanding of the growth of nationalism in one small part of Africa.

The bulk of the research on which this essay is based was carried out between 1962 and 1964, when I was a member of the staff of what was then Makerere University College and later of Nairobi University College. I am grateful to both institutions and also to the University of Manchester, who financed my secondment to Nairobi, for their assistance. During that period I made regular visits to Northern Uganda, in the course of which I collected a good deal of material in interviews with a wide range of people including the party founders, party supporters, chiefs, councillors, and local authority officials, Members of Parliament, civil servants, and church officials. I am grateful for the generous assistance they gave me in understanding the political history of the area between the end of the Second World War and independence.

In addition to this oral evidence, I was also able to draw considerably upon documentary sources at district level which had hitherto scarcely been tapped by researchers. These are the district records of both the provincial administration and the African local governments, which in the case of Lango and Acholi Districts provided a rich, if uneven, store of archival material previously neglected. My first task was, in fact, to sort out and tidy up those records, which had lain untouched in district stores for some time. I am grateful to the Government of Uganda for permission to use those archives.

Documentary and oral sources at district level were augmented by material in the central government archives related to developments in local government institutions over the period under review. I am also grateful for permission to use those archives and for the unfailing assistance given me by those in charge of the records at Entebbe. I am also grateful for permission to use certain selected files in the then Ministry of Regional Administration.[7]

In 1962 I served as a member of an Archives Committee set up by the then Prime Minister to ascertain the position regarding district archives. While that position gave me no special access to records, it did

enable me to see—as indeed the work of the committee established—
that Uganda's district archives at that time were a rich source of study
material. Unfortunately difficulties of staff and storage made it impossible to move the records to a central repository, and political
events in Uganda during subsequent years have further impeded a
solution to the problem of preservation. I sincerely hope, however,
that even now it will be possible to save those records, which offer
a store of information about Uganda's more recent past.

In the course of the years, and particularly in the period when I
was actively engaged in research in Northern Uganda, I have incurred
deep debts to very many people for their assistance and friendship.
While it is impossible to name them all, I must thank especially the
former President of Uganda, Dr Milton Obote, who gave me my first
introduction to Lango; Mr Eric Lakidi, Mr Peter Oola, Mr Alex Ojera,
Mr Alex Latim, and Mr Obonyo, who respectively helped me to understand Acholi's political parties; and Miss Mildred Brown, of Boroboro
Mission, Lira, who over the years gave me much hospitality and
assisted me with interpreters. Central government officials and political
leaders from other regions were also generous in the time they gave
to discussing with me the whole issue of central-local relations,
thus enabling me to see Northern Uganda more properly in the perspective of the whole country. Professor A. Southall, then of Makerere
University College, introduced me to West Nile, and Professor Colin
Leys, then also of Makerere, more than once read drafts of the manuscript. Professor B. Webster, Professor of History at Makerere
University Kampala, helped me to eliminate some of my early mis-
takes on Acholi traditional history. I am also grateful to Professor Colin
Leys and the East African Publishing House for permission to re-
produce the map on page xii. Finally, I must thank the Director of the
Institute of Commonwealth Studies, University of London, Professor
W. H. Morris-Jones, for the facilities given me when I was a visiting
Fellow in 1969, during which time this study was finally written.
Without that period of quiet in his Institute, this monograph would
never have been completed.

I alone, of course, remain responsible for the final conclusions
reached. My one regret is that those who helped me with their ideas,
information, and opinions have had to wait so long for this manuscript, which has been delayed by numerous other responsibilities.
I can only hope that they will accept it even at this late date and that
it may contribute something to our understanding of the political
development of Uganda and the events of the last decade.

*Lusaka*                                                          C.G.

# POSTSCRIPT PRIOR TO PUBLICATION

Between the completion of this manuscript and its publication Uganda has been the scene of many dramatic changes following the military coup of January 1971 which put General Idi Amin Dada into power, forcing former President Milton Obote into exile. Tragically, one of the consequences of the intense upheavals that have followed that coup has been the disappearance or death of a significant number of Uganda's former political leaders, including many to whom my own debt is considerable, for the way in which they helped me to understand Uganda, and some of whom figure in the pages of this essay. Perhaps this brief essay on one aspect of Uganda's nationalist development in the 1950s and early 1960s may stand therefore as a small tribute to the part they played in building independent Uganda.

*Lusaka*
*July 1973*

C.G.

# CONTENTS

MAP
*page xii*

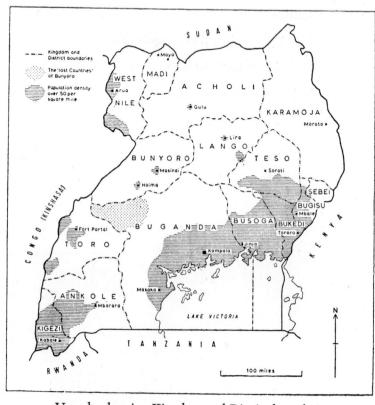

Uganda, showing Kingdom and District boundaries

Reproduced from Colin Leys, *Politicians and Policies*, East African Publishing
House, Nairobi, 1967

# INTRODUCTION

Situated in the heart of Africa, straddled across the Equator, five hundred miles from the sea, covering an area of 93,981 square miles, Uganda is rich in contrasts and of great physical beauty. The country ranges from the lush and fertile northern shores of Lake Victoria to the semi-desert area of Karamoja in the north. Most of it is plateau, ranging from 3,000 to 4,500 feet above sea level, and although it lies in the tropics the altitude and the moderating influence of Lake Victoria ensure for the most part equable temperatures. The people are predominantly agriculturists, small-scale peasant farmers combining subsistence with production of cash crops, although there is a significant section of pastoralists in the northern half of the country. In 1963, a year after independence, agriculture, forestry, and fishing still accounted for more than 60 per cent of the country's national income. During the 1950s a small but significant industrial base was built up at Jinja and Kampala but agriculture, based on peasant production, provided the mainstay of the economy. The country remained primarily dependent on its two major cash crops of coffee and cotton.

The country is for administrative purposes divided into eighteen districts, most conforming to tribal divisions. Formerly these districts were grouped together into the four Provinces of Buganda, Eastern, Western, and Northern. Since 1962 the provincial level has for administrative purposes been abandoned and the district remains the main unit of government. Until 1962 the province was however an important intermediary level between centre and district.

Uganda's peoples form a rich plural society, with considerable ethnic variation. There was never a large settler population and Europeans and Asians in the colonial period were few in number. The African population (just under six and a half million in 1959, ten million ten years later) is divided into four linguistic categories: Bantu, Nilote, Paranilote (Itesot, Karamoja, and Kakwa, formerly known as Nilo-Hamitic), and Sudanic speakers (including Lugbara and Madi). The largest single ethnic group are the Ganda, who occupy the central, most fertile, part of the country. The distribution of the population varies considerably, from the densely populated areas of

Busoga, Kigezi, and Buganda, which in places have a population density of over 800, to the open, sparsely populated areas of the north. The population of the four provinces in 1948 and 1959 was as follows:[1]

|  | Population | | | | Density per square mile | |
|  | 1948 | | 1959 | | 1948 | 1959 |
|---|---|---|---|---|---|---|
|  |  | % |  | % |  |  |
| Buganda | 1,302,162 | 26.5 | 1,834,128 | 28.4 | 81 | 114 |
| Eastern | 1,508,572 | 30.7 | 1,872,949 | 29.0 | 137 | 171 |
| Northern | 943,175 | 19.2 | 1,244,871 | 19.3 | 28 | 39 |
| Western | 1,163,706 | 23.7 | 1,497,510 | 23.2 | 67 | 87 |

Traditional political structures varied from the centralized autocracy of Buganda to the decentralized stateless structure of Iteso and Bakigo. The four Bantu kingdoms of Buganda, Bunyoro, Toro, and Ankole each had a centralized state structure (most developed in Buganda), a rich tradition, and a ruler who symbolized above all the kingdom's and the people's identity. Their Treaty Agreements, made with the incoming British at the turn of the century, accorded them a status different from that of the other tribal groups in the non-treaty districts, although only in the case of Buganda did this reflect any genuine autonomy. Two features dominated Uganda politics in the decade before independence. First, the most important political division up to independence (and indeed until 1967) was that between Buganda and 'the rest'. Closely related to this was, second, a characteristic emphasis upon local institutions. There was a considerable emphasis on local government by both colonial authorities and politically articulate leaders.

Many observers have commented on the absence of any country-wide political organization in Uganda before the late 1950s and the apparent difficulties that political parties had in establishing a national organization through which local dissatisfactions could be channelled into political activity.[2] One of the major features of the political scene up to 1960 was indeed the absence of any party organization that drew the whole country together. The Wild Report pointed in 1959 to the difficulties the existing parties had faced in establishing a country-wide organization, concluding that it was scarcely to be wondered at that the parties did not then 'present a picture of united leadership, carefully thought out positive policies and fully developed branch organizations'.[3] The history of the parties appears to bear this out. The first nationalist party, the Uganda National Congress (UNC), formed by I. K. Musazi and Abu Mayanja in Buganda in 1952, foundered in that Province essentially because of opposition from the Buganda government. Its national organization was bedevilled by problems of internal party leadership; it suffered three major leadership upheavals between 1953 and 1959, out of which Milton Obote (who had entered the Legislative Council as Lango representative at the beginning of 1958) emerged in 1959 in control of its dominant wing, consisting primarily of Northern and Eastern Province supporters. The Uganda People's Congress (UPC), founded in 1960, was fundamentally the lineal descendant of the UNC, formed out of a merger of Obote's wing of the UNC and the Uganda People's Union (UPU), the latter an alliance of non-Ganda, non-UNC members of the Legislative Council formed after the elections of 1958. The second major party to emerge was the Democratic Party (DP). Also formed in Buganda, in 1954, the DP was in the first place concerned primarily with the position of Catholics in Buganda and remained primarily associated in the popular mind with the Catholic Church. As the Buganda government grew increasingly isolationist in the late 1950s, however, the DP also came to represent those Ganda opposed to the entrenchment of a neo-traditionalist regime, and thus stood for the progressive element in Buganda. From 1955 onwards branches were established in other districts but like the UNC the DP failed before 1959 to create a country-wide organization.

The slow development of country-wide party machinery was attributed by the Wild Committee in part to the late introduction of direct elections, for which the parties would be forced to organize on a national basis. If one of the decisive factors in the development of political parties in African states has been the devolution by the colonial authorities of a meaningful measure of power, and the introduction of institutions and procedures such as an electoral system which makes it technically possible to seek power constitutionally,[4] then the fact that in Uganda the first country-wide direct elections were not held until 1961 must be given considerable weight in explaining the slow development of political parties. The first four Africans to enter the Legislative Council in 1945 were nominated by the Governor. At that time the Council seemed 'to have little interest in the African mind as a forum for public discussion'.[5] The number was increased to eight in 1950 and to fifteen in 1953; those representatives were elected indirectly, first by the Provincial Councils set up in 1949, and after 1953 by the District Councils. Constitutional changes in 1955 established a ministerial system and put Ugandans into the Executive Council but it was only in 1958 that the first direct elections for the legislature took place, in eleven districts. The first general election, as a result of which the Legislative Council became predominantly an elected body, took place in 1961. Internal self-government followed in May 1961. In 1962 the Legislative Council was replaced by a fully elected National Assembly, with Prime Minister and Cabinet drawn from the majority party. The second general election in April 1962 put Dr Obote, leader of the UPC, into office as Prime Minister. The country became independent in the following October.

Country-wide elections for which parties had to organize were thus introduced late, relative to the achievement of independence, and as a result the parties were slow to acquire a genuine national organization. The experience of Uganda's neighbour, what was then Tanganyika, suggests, however, that this alone could scarcely explain the situation. Tanganyika's first general election in 1958 found the Tanganyika African National Union (TANU) already established. Thus the late introduction of country-wide elections must be viewed as only one, if in this case highly significant, variable. In the Ugandan context there were also other significant contributory factors, including the late (in relation to independence) emergence of full-time politicians at the centre. Again a comparison with Tanganyika and Kenya makes the point. What is relevant here, however, is that the consequence was that until 1960 political parties could not be regarded as major institutions of national integration. While nationally-orientated leaders in the Legislative Council argued about central institutions, much of the focus of popular political interest was local until a short time before independence.

The absence of elections and the slow growth of political parties are not the only factors to be taken into account in explaining the characteristic focus of politics over these years. The most critical problem throughout the 1950s was not the question of African representation, or even self-government, but that of Buganda separatism, which in its most extreme form threatened to pull the country apart. It is therefore essential to say something about Buganda in this period.

The kingdom of Buganda, the largest single ethnic area, enjoying provincial status, rich, more economically developed than any other part of the country, proud and conscious of a separate identity, rejected the idea of a close association with the rest of the country and any direct participation in the central government. This Ganda separatism had its roots in the Buganda Agreement of 1900 and the special treatment and status then accorded to the kingdom. It was intensified by the deportation of the Kabaka in November 1953 and the crises that followed. The new Buganda Agreement of 1955 which enabled the Kabaka to return and ended the crisis also gave Buganda a much greater degree of independence of the centre than she had previously enjoyed. Between 1955 and 1962, therefore, the main task that faced politicians and colonial administrators alike was to evolve a constitutional structure that would preserve the country's unity, give it the strong central government generally recognized as necessary, but at the same time overcome Buganda's not surprising reluctance to forfeit the position she had won. This was made all the more difficult by the increasingly isolationist attitude adopted by those in power in Buganda.[6]

After a very brief honeymoon period in 1956 the Buganda government, dominated by the neo-traditionalist and strongly isolationist element, increasingly withdrew from the centre and questioned proposed constitutional changes for the country as a whole. They rejected direct elections to the Legislative Council in 1956; withdrew from that body in 1958; boycotted the 1958 elections; refused in 1959 to participate in the Committee set up to investigate constitutional reform,[7] and in 1960 cold-shouldered the Munster Commission of Inquiry set up to look into future relationships between each part of the country and the centre. In the same years a strongly populist Ganda movement, the Uganda National Movement, emerged which, while in conflict with the Buganda 'establishment' nevertheless rejected any association with the central government. The experience of the National Movement of 1959 and its successful institution of a boycott of Asian traders showed the strength of its grass roots support, as did the electoral victory of the Ganda Kabaka Yekka in the Lukiko elections of 1961.

In 1961 Buganda boycotted the first country-wide elections. By that time, however, her leaders had been forced by events elsewhere in the country (and especially by the results of the elections) to recognize the need for political compromise. With remarkable speed they negotiated a rapprochement with the UPC that effectively enabled Uganda to move to independence but also won Buganda the quasi-federal position she had demanded.[8]

The country weathered this succession of crises, including the boycott and Buganda's attempt to secede in December 1960, but not surprisingly the Munster Commission reported in 1961 that 'It is hardly too much to say that every serious problem that we encountered in Uganda had its roots in the Buganda problem'.[9]

This concentration upon Buganda in the years before independence greatly influenced the evolving pattern of local-central relations, so far as the other districts were concerned, particularly during the 1950s. Although Buganda's attitude was not uniformly separatist in this decade, her position as the largest single unit within an independent Uganda, and her future relationship with the rest of the country, were the key issues of the period, which created an acute conflict in internal politics about the distribution of power at the centre. Non-Ganda leaders refused to accept the idea of a 'state within a state'[10] on which it appeared to them that British policy had hitherto been based. Local leaders in the districts they represented were equally adamant in their demands for a full share in central power. The non-Ganda leadership could thus draw on local support at the periphery to give added weight to their campaign in the Legislative Council. They turned to their own constituents to reinforce their case. To sustain their position at the local level they had, however, to ensure continued local support, which meant in turn championing local issues and demands. Local interests thus had to be taken carefully into account. As a result the local arena was an important focus of politics and to a large extent the question of power at the centre was debated at that level. Local-central relations were therefore conducted within a number of separate local arenas, all linked through the association at the national level of their national representatives.[11]

Until 1960 neither the UNC nor the DP had been able to establish a viable country-wide party machine. Nevertheless, the results of the first general elections in April 1961 demonstrated massive support for both parties. Throughout the country outside Buganda the poll was generally high, in some constituencies as high as 95 per cent.[12] This massive support was repeated in the second general election the following year. Of the 59 seats contested outside Buganda, the UPC won 37 with 537,598 votes, the DP 22 with 474,256 votes. The percentage poll again ranged as high as 90 per cent. The elections therefore indicated the existence of strong popular support for the two parties,[13] which proved crucial in forcing the Ganda to negotiate. The abstention of the Ganda in the 1961 elections gave victory to the DP which formed the first African government. This led the Ganda, highly antagonistic towards the Catholic-dominated DP, to change their tactics and to enter the electoral battle in alliance with the UPC.

The formation in May 1962 of the first government in which the UPC was the dominant partner was determined by the Lukiko electoral victory of that party's ally, Kabaka Yekka, which in the previous February had polled 600,000 votes and won all but three of the seats. Nevertheless the national elections provided the political parties, and especially the UPC, with the popular support that proved their major strength during the negotiations of these two years.

The parties' major weakness, however, was their failure to win any support within Buganda. The absence of Ganda support for political parties beyond the handful of people who voted for the DP in 1961 was a consequence of the long conflict of the 1950s between party leaders and the Buganda government which had destroyed any popular party base. This reached its logical conclusion when at the end of 1960 the Ganda established their own political party, Kabaka Yekka (KY), which combined all the political groupings in Buganda except the DP. It was a Ganda national movement and, with the throne as its symbol, it trounced all opposition to win a resounding victory in the first direct elections to the Lukiko in February 1962. While the alliance between KY and UPC provided the way for the Ganda to rejoin the centre, it did not provide the UPC with a base in Buganda.

The final constitutional settlement of September 1962 gave Buganda the federal status she had demanded and permitted her to elect her representatives to the National Assembly indirectly through the Lukiko. It also however gave the other districts significant political gains which reflected the extent to which those districts remained the focus of political interest. The rest of the country outside Buganda, on paper at least, also benefited from the settlement in terms of increased status and power, which the preoccupation with Buganda should not lead us to overlook.

Only Toro, of the other districts of Uganda, had since 1953 consistently demanded federal status. Other districts had proposed a unitary state. Nevertheless, the district, in the final independence settlement, acquired political resources that might not normally be associated with local governments in a unitary state.

These gains can be summarized briefly. First, the western kingdoms of Toro, Ankole, and Bunyoro, whose rulers had always enjoyed a distinctive status (although no additional power) on the basis of their Agreements, were granted the full federal relationship that had earlier been refused. Second, Busoga district was granted the same federal relationship as the western kingdoms, and was accorded the title of Territory.[14] The status thus acquired was more significant than the legislative authority, although the latter might, depending upon the interpretation of 'traditional and customary matters', have proved wider than was originally intended. Nevertheless, the constitutional position was conceded where it had earlier been denied. The political importance of the settlement was indicated by the Prime Minister's personal intervention in the negotiations. Third, the non-Agreement districts obtained important political offices which might have been thought inappropriate to local government bodies. They were permitted, if they wished, to establish the post of ceremonial district head;

as all except Teso and West Nile did. Every district council retained an
elected chairman, who did not necessarily have to be an elected member of the council. All councils were given the right to style up to four
of their committee chairmen ministers (a provision which the Munster
Commission had recommended for Toro alone).[15] This politicization
of the local authorities was not disturbed by subsequent changes in the
local government structure by which the UPC/KY government between 1963 and 1965 began to tighten central government control
over the district administration.[16] The provision of political offices
at district level was therefore apparently regarded by national leaders
as important, and suggested the significance of the district as a locus
of influence. Political officers at the head of the local authorities were
moreover retained after the crisis of May 1966, when the collision
between Buganda and the central government led to the abolition of
that kingdom as a separate entity. Although the new local government
legislation of 1967 established very firm central control over district
institutions, it did not disturb the status of the district hierarchy
itself.[17]

To understand the basis of this district influence upon the nationalist
leaders over this period it is essential to look at the growth of politics
at the district level during the years before independence. In the
rest of this monograph we shall be concerned with such developments
in two districts of Northern Uganda, Lango and Acholi.

# 2

# NORTHERN UGANDA:
# THE BACKGROUND TO THE 1950s

Events in Uganda since independence have increasingly highlighted apparent divergences between the 'north' and the 'south', and many observers have seen this as the major political division in the country. Whether or not this has been the basis of recent political cleavages, the northern parts of Uganda were in 1950 certainly thought of by many Africans and Europeans in southern Uganda as cut off from the rest of the country, remote and different.

The Northern Province of Uganda, reconstituted in 1947, consisted of the districts of West Nile (including Madi), Acholi, Lango, and Karamoja. Stretching away to the Sudan and Congo borders with a total area of 33,168 square miles, the province is the largest in Uganda; although in the 1940s it had the fastest growing population, it was the least densely populated and the least economically developed. In 1964 it still had a *per capita* income well below the national average. It is a predominantly Nilotic area, dominated by the major Nilotic tribes, Alur, Acholi, Lango, Jonam, Labwor and Nyakwai, of whom in 1942 Lord Hailey had written: 'the independent and equalitarian spirit of these tribes is conspicuous'.[1] The varied and complex population in West Nile includes Lugbara and Kakwa as well as Alur. In Karamoja, very much less developed, are the Paranilotic groups of Jie, Dodoth, and Karamojong. In the 1940s and 1950s the non-African population was less than a thousand, consisting of Asians in trade and in the cotton industry, and European missionaries and government officials.

Away from the highland areas of West Nile, it is rolling savannah country: a vast, undulating, grassy tableland broken by rocky outcrops and long ranges of hills 'like the backs of crouching animals', studded with acacias and in some places borassus palms. Most of the area enjoys an equable climate, which becomes hotter and drier towards the Sudan border and the lowlands of the Nile valley and the Nile itself, flowing sluggishly through Madi country. The rainfall is less reliable and its soil less fertile than in the south and south-eastern parts of the country. Its river systems, which drain off south to the Lake Kyoga-Lake Kwania complex and west into Lake Albert, are in most parts seasonal but water supplies have been greatly improved by the system of boreholes introduced into the area, on which today many people depend.

There is considerable variation in the quality of the land, as well as in the rainfall. Good arable land with relatively high rainfall lies in the triangle between Gula, Lira, and Kitgum, and consequently a large percentage of the population is found in those areas. Surrounding these regions of relatively high rainfall there are belts of moderately good land but the whole of East Madi, the lowlands of West Nile, the country in the east of Acholi beyond Kitgum, and in the south-west of Acholi, is poor. The result is considerable variation in population density, highest in parts of Lango and West Nile, with 57 to the square mile, but as low as 19 in Acholi.

In the years up to independence land was still held generally under traditional tenure which provided considerable security (but not freehold ownership) for the individual. Generally there was no land shortage, with the exception of one or two small areas in Lango and West Nile.

The people of the north (with the exception of the Karimojong) are predominantly agriculturists and cattle herdsmen, in most cases with a small plot for subsistence, some cash crops, and some cattle. The major cash crops in the 1940s and 1950s were cotton and tobacco, cattle exports also being important. The acreage of land under food crops increased steadily after the Second World War (not least because of the increasing population) but cash crop production also increased, particularly in response to the improved crop prices after 1952.

Increased production, which began in the late 1940s, brought more cash into the area. The Annual Report for the Northern Province in 1949 reported that one of the most marked features of the year had been the 'unprecedented amount of cash' that had found its way into people's hands, especially those of primary producers. In Lango the cash income from cotton increased from £140,000 in 1948 to £504,000 in 1949. The income from other cash crops was £2,290 and income from other sources included £64,000 from the sale of cattle and hides, £20,000 as an estimate of wages paid out by Protectorate government departments, and £40,000 from the local government. The cash return for the main exports from West Nile—cotton, tobacco, hides—was £180,000 in 1949.[2]

Between 1952 and 1954 overall production increased by 50,000 tons for the area as a whole. There was also an increase in tobacco growing, particularly among the returned ex-servicemen in West Acholi, although that development was hampered by restricted facilities for curing. The overall increase in the amount of cash consequently available to producers is indicated by the value of cash crops and exports of subsistence crops between 1949 and 1954.[3] Lango's cotton exports and cattle trade south across Lake Kyoga to Buganda made it the most prosperous district in the province. But clearly all three enjoyed development in this period.

|  | Lango £ | Acholi £ | West Nile £ |
|---|---|---|---|
| 1949 | 527,482 | 242,875 | 159,412 |
| 1952 | 1,012,285 | 655,398 | 375,390 |
| 1953 | 653,902 | 382,037 | 261,843 |
| 1954 | 864,557 | 466,736 | 503,645 |

Generally, however, notwithstanding this increased production, there was in the early 1950s a considerable unexploited agricultural potential in the north. Agricultural development was slowed down by several factors: lack of wage labour, due in part to the small population; inadequate numbers of agricultural extension staff in the area; poor internal communications; lack of incentive because of the limited availability of consumer goods. Development in trade and commerce was also slow and fluctuating. Early post-war attempts by ex-servicemen to establish themselves in trade did not prove very successful, nor early attempts at cooperatives. A Lango Shopkeepers' Cooperative Society started in 1946 faded out of existence by 1950. Two African bus companies in the same district foundered for lack of capital and business acumen.[4] The Acholi Bus Company started by Erisa Lakor in West Acholi, the Kitgum Bus Company started by ex-servicemen in East Acholi, and the Chua Express, all suffered the same fate. In West Nile there was a short burst of economic activity following the return of ex-servicemen to the district, which faded away, and then in the early 1950s a slow, limited expansion of trade began again.[5]

The increased cash in circulation did not result in any considerable expansion in commerce. Although Gulu and Lira both grew fairly rapidly, the province was characterized by a marked absence of internal trade. The population was dependent for the purchase of consumer goods on the small shopkeepers along the main roads and in the county centres, and 'barter traders' who walked and cycled to village markets. None of these offered a great variety of goods; indeed most traders and storekeepers restricted their stocks to basic necessities. This slow development of retail trade was due to a combination of factors, all relevant to the slow development of the north, including limited local capital resources, problems of internal communications, and the absence of extensive credit facilities and local wholesale facilities. The Northern Province was consequently in 1956 still 'an area in the development of which commercial enterprise has so far played only a negligible part'.[6] In commerce as in agriculture there was considerable room for expansion. A report on Northern Uganda in 1956 suggested that 'in Lango, for instance, between 20 per cent and 25 per cent of the known annual cash income of the population cannot be accounted for through normal trade channels, and we were told of cases in Acholi where porters had failed through lack of interest to collect their monthly wages'.[7] Money was spent on cows, bride price, school fees, and much, it was suggested, was hoarded.

Limited communications were partially responsible for slow commercial development. Within each district roads were generally poor. Arterial roads were good but communication between north and south was considerably slowed down by the river crossings across the Nile. The railway stopped at Soroti; the northern extension to Lira was not finally opened until 1962, and further extended through Acholi to Pakwach in 1969. The road journey via Mbale and Soroti to Gulu and then on to West Nile was long and dusty. The more direct communications through Buganda and Bunyoro involved crossing the Nile by ferry at Atura, Pakwach, and Laropi, or across Lake Kyogo.[8] For the people of Acholi and Lango, their easiest and most used line of communication was east to Mbale which was only a day's journey by road from Gulu. It was to Mbale, and to a lesser extent to Soroti, that northern traders went for their goods, although some Lango in the southern part of that district made frequent excursions across the lake into the Bulemezi and Buruli areas of Buganda. Water transport was vital for moving the cotton and other crops south to Buganda and Busoga buying points.

Every year a large labour force crossed by ferry from West Nile south to Buganda to look for work. Fewer migrants went south from Lango and Acholi than from West Nile, and those who did tended to work for the government rather than for the Ganda.[9] There were two separate lines of communication: from West Nile men went south through Bunyoro to Buganda itself; from Lango and Acholi communication was primarily to the eastern districts and down to Mbale, although the southern part of Lango also had contacts across the lake with Buganda. Only a small proportion of the total population did in fact move beyond the district, even in the mid-fifties. These migrants, however, provided links between the northern and southern parts of the Protectorate. There was among northerners more awareness of events taking place in the south than might have been thought, although the population 'generally appeared to be concerned only with its own small circle'.[10] People knew of events in Kenya and in 1955 they were not slow to become aware of the revolt in the Southern Sudan. The Church provided considerable opportunities for communicating especially with Buganda and the Eastern Province. The region was not therefore entirely isolated.

The rate of educational development in the north had distinctly lagged behind the southern parts of Uganda, particularly Buganda, and generally there was a much smaller number of men and women with higher education in these districts than in the south. Gulu had two good secondary schools (one at the Protestant and one at the Catholic mission); Lira a junior secondary school; West Nile a senior secondary school at Nyapea, started in 1940. Some boys found their way to schools in the south such as Nabumali in Mbale, or Mwiri College near Jinja. But only a handful of young men from the north had reached Makerere before 1950. In this respect Acholi was better off than the other northern districts, since 21 Acholi had gone through Makerere before 1950, compared with seven from Lango and three from West Nile. No Lango student went overseas before 1950. In the early 1950s a number of young Acholi moved on from Makerere to universities abroad. A few also found their way to the Sudan. But overall the number of men or women with secondary or higher education was very small. The contrast between north and south is highlighted by the statistics: of a total of 1,912 pupils in senior secondary schools in the Protectorate in 1952, only 151 were from the Northern Province. Of 3,605 children in junior secondary schools only 501 were from the north; and only 22,740 of a total of 173,000 children in primary school. These figures reflected the smaller population but they also indicated the poorer educational facilities, at all levels, in the north.[11]

The Northern Province, in particular Acholi District, had supplied large numbers of men for the armed forces during the Second World War, who had returned with a new knowledge of the outside world. These men had generally settled down after their service abroad with remarkable speed, most returning to their own land. They were not, it seemed, the force for political change that ex-servicemen have often been assumed to be in post-war Africa, although in Acholi some of them certainly became active in party affairs.[12]

Interest in local affairs was however suggested by a letter written by a group of Lango soldiers in transit camp in 1946 to the Lango Native Council asking why Lango did not have a secretary-general as Teso did.[13] Moreover the existence of a generalized, even if not informed, interest in political events in the Protectorate and elsewhere is suggested by the awareness of events taking place in the neighbouring territory of Kenya in the early 1950s. The Emergency in that territory aroused considerable apprehension at possible repercussions in Uganda, particularly as regards land.[14] People feared its alienation to Europeans.

Over northern Uganda as a whole there seemed to exist after the Second World War a muted but general rural discontent. Administrative reports of the late forties and early fifties acknowledged a lack of confidence in the colonial government among the people and a pronounced suspicion of anything concerning land.[15] Although there was no shortage of land, the Protectorate government's policy on forest reserves, which generally required the consent of district councils for implementation, encountered strong opposition. There were economic grievances about government policies concerning crop prices and crop marketing, and I. K. Musazi, the Ganda politician, was well received when he went north in 1951 to establish branches of his Federation of Uganda African Farmers.[16]. This economic discontent did not, however, assume serious proportions; it was certainly not on the scale of the rural discontent that had erupted into violence in Buganda in 1945 and 1949. It lost a good deal of its force with the improved prices of the 1950s. There was a small strike among African local government employees in Lira in 1952 and a second (unconnected) strike in Gulu in 1953 but neither proved to be the prelude to any sustained agitation against the central government.[17] Northern Uganda's reactions against the colonial presence in the years up to 1953 had been restrained. Nowhere in the province was there anything that could be termed serious rural resistance to alien rule. A handful of voluntary associations had been established but these, such as the Young Lango Association and the Acholi Association, were representative of the new, younger, educated element who wanted to participate in rather than break the system.[18] Before the Uganda National Congress was formed in 1952 northern Uganda was not in a political ferment; this was in part because the popular grievances that elsewhere in Africa played a vital part in the articulation of a successful nationalist movement had not reached the surface. The social pre-conditions for wider political consciousness had scarcely appeared. In northern Uganda in the post-war years (as indeed elsewhere in Uganda) there was nothing of the large-scale African assertion against the colonial presence that has been associated with the growth of African nationalism.[19] There was, however, a considerable development in the institutions of local government. These developments, which were a result of the overall official emphasis on local government district institutions in these years, are best understood in the light of the general evolution of local administration over the period, to which we must now turn.

# 3

## THE EVOLUTION OF
## LOCAL ADMINISTRATION

Earlier it was suggested that the focus upon the problem of Buganda and her position vis-à-vis the rest of the country forced other Ugandan politicians at the centre, and especially the representative members in the Legislative Council, to pay careful attention to their links with the localities from which their support was drawn. The most important local arena to emerge for these local-central relations was within the local government institutions at the district level.

The district assumed this prominence largely because there were by the 1950s district institutions through which support could be canvassed. During these years the creation of representative local government institutions, enjoying a good deal of patronage and responsible for the allocation of considerable resources in the way of local services, emphasized the district as a significant level at which to seek political power. The growth of local government provided a set of institutions at district level within which it was possible to challenge the colonial authorities for control. Not surprisingly therefore local level politics focused largely on these local government bodies the foundations of which had been built over a considerable period of time. Thus the situation was not, as some observers re-marked, one in which there was no nationalist political activity outside Buganda. Political activity was rather focused on the district as a level at which power could be won. A study of politics at the district level in the country outside Buganda must of necessity therefore focus first on the growth of local administration in these years.

The administrative system that had been built up in Uganda by 1945 emphasized the district (which was in many but not all cases synonymous with an ethnic unit) as the basic unit of control and governmental activity.[1] Within the district the District Commissioner stood at the apex of the administrative structure. Responsible to the Provincial Commissioner above him, he exercised his authority through a hierarchy of salaried chiefs at county, sub-county, and parish level, who together formed the native administration.

The structure of the native administration in the districts outside Buganda closely followed the Ganda hierarchy of chiefs that the

British had found in action when they assumed control over that kingdom. The model was however significantly modified in certain respects. The chiefs came more completely under the control of the provincial administration than was the case in Buganda, primarily because there was no intermediate government comparable to the Buganda government, and no paramount chief like the Kabaka.[2] The status of rulers of the western kingdoms did not in this case give them comparable authority. Chiefs did not, furthermore, enjoy the use of official estates as did their counterparts in Buganda, so that there was not the same close connection between political and economic power that formed the basis of the Ganda political structure. Chiefs did emerge as a privileged economic class, not because of their control of land but rather because of the advantages they acquired as a result of regular salaries. (By 1954, for example, county chiefs in Acholi earned between £285 and £465.[3]) This enabled them to move more rapidly than others into the money economy, to build their houses, develop their homesteads, educate their children, and grow cash crops.

The statutory basis of the chiefs' authority was the Native Authority Ordinance of 1919. Subsequent amendments under the Ordinance empowered chiefs to issue orders on a wide range of matters that directly affected the rural population. The law also made them responsible to the Governor through the provincial administration for law and order within their area. Their authority was further increased from the early 1940s onwards as their responsibilities were enlarged, especially in relation to the enforcement of agricultural bye-laws and of rules for improved farming, such as soil conservation measures. The chiefs were thus, in their capacity as the native authority, tax collectors, guardians of law and order, interpreters of government policy, and agents of development. They were responsible for the maintenance of a wide range of local services, including roads, buildings, and health facilities. They had the right to order men in the local community to provide unpaid labour for a variety of local services. They also enjoyed powers of arrest for a wide range of offences. They exercised judicial powers sitting as native courts at district, county, and sub-county level. They were consequently a powerful body of men, particularly at the more senior levels, who constituted a powerful local executive. To back them up they had the authority of the provincial administration and the police.[4]

This native administration did not differ significantly from that in other British territories in so far as its powers and functions were concerned. It was different in that the men appointed as chiefs did not in most cases derive their authority from a position within a traditional political structure. The chief in Uganda was not (and this was equally true of Kenya) a traditional ruler as was his counterpart in Tanganyika, Nyasaland, or Northern Rhodesia. In some districts some chiefs could claim a traditional status. In the 1930s, in Acholi at least, the provincial administration attempted to use the traditional political unit (which they termed a clan but which is more properly described as a chiefdom) as the basis for administration. But from 1940 onwards this experiment was abandoned and, certainly in the eyes of the administration, chiefs were appointed as civil servants. It is true they were also part of a system modelled on one elsewhere in Uganda (Buganda) that had traditional foundations; nevertheless their role was essentially that of the modern civil servant.

A further difference arose out of the relationship between chiefs and councils. The chief was linked to a council system that was intended as a check upon the native administration in a much more direct manner than in other territories. The council system as it developed in Uganda seems to have been almost unique, certainly in East Africa. Councils to assist the chief as native authority were established in other British territories in the post-war period but they do not appear to have taken root in the way they did in Uganda or to have acted as a comparable check upon the native administration. Two further contrasts were, first, the extent to which the Uganda councils included an element of popular representation and, second, the extent to which that popular element rapidly used the councils as a forum to express local grievances.[5]

It is worth looking back at the origins of the councils. The Protectorate government had established in the 1920s (and in some cases before) a district council in each district, consisting of county and sub-county chiefs. Those councils enjoyed no legislative powers; they had only the right, subject to the Governor's pleasure, to alter native law and custom, and to fix penalties for its breach. Thus they enjoyed no actual power or authority. Then in the mid-thirties the provincial administration had experimented by introducing an unofficial element into the councils. The reason for this was official alarm at the growing gap between chiefs and people and concern at what was regarded as the chiefs' increasingly authoritarian behaviour. The experiment began in the Eastern Province, where there was also a newly emergent younger element among the people who had expressed dissatisfaction with the chiefs. In 1937 in Teso district a new chain of councils was set up at each administrative level, in which nominated unofficials as well as chiefs took a place.[6] By 1940 the provincial administration and the Governor, Philip Mitchell, had reached agreement on the need to ensure that the system of councils for the Eastern Province should generally become 'increasingly representative of local opinion'. The experiment was extended to the Northern Province in 1943 and generally throughout the Protectorate at the end of the War. Although some administrators were looking for men with a traditional authority to act as local representatives, all of them were obviously seeking to bring new men into the system and to make the councils representative of the community as a whole. Thus the Eastern Province *muruka* (parish) councils, for example, included 'three schoolmasters elected by the rest of the council'; and it was reported 'On every grade of Council there is a large unofficial majority and as far as possible every type and grade of society is represented. The District and Provincial Commissioner's nominations ensure that no particularly able African is left out.'[7]

By 1950 this council system had been established throughout the Protectorate, with the unofficials elected through a system of indirect elections starting at the parish level. The composition of the councils varied slightly from district to district. In some, but not all, an attempt was made to revive traditional leadership. Notwithstanding local variations in membership, however, by 1949 the general pattern was the same throughout the country. Every district had a chain of councils from parish to district level which provided an opportunity for both the ordinary peasant and the new educated group, such as teachers, to participate in local affairs through discussions with the chiefs. Election to the lowest, parish, council was by acclamation at a meeting of all local male taxpayers. Election to the councils above was indirect, each council acting as an electoral college for the council above. Thus the parish council was of great importance in the system, since it was through it that a large section of the non-official element found its way into the superior councils. At each level the chiefs were expected to cooperate with their councils, which had the right to discuss those matters for which the native administration was responsible. The councils were nevertheless purely advisory and lacked any executive powers.[8]

The Uganda African Local Government Ordinance of 1949 gave a statutory basis to this council system. It provided in each district for an *African Local Government* consisting of the *Chiefs and the District Council*. The chiefs, although they continued to be appointed by the Protectorate government, became the executive of this African local government. The District Commissioner withdrew from the chairmanship of the district council; the chairman was henceforth one of the county chiefs elected by the district council from among their ranks. Statutory recognition was also given to three senior officers for each African local government, Secretary-General, Treasurer, and

District Judge, all also nominated by the district council from among the county chiefs.[9]

The Ordinance did not assign to the district councils any specific powers but left the Governor to prescribe their constitutions, membership, and functions. The councils were permitted to make byelaws on matters over which the chiefs had powers but these had to be approved by the Provincial Commissioner. The District Commissioner furthermore, appointed council committees. Thus to all intents and purposes under law the district councils still enjoyed only deliberative and advisory functions. Nevertheless the legal recognition that they now received added considerably to their standing in the district. Moreover the fact that district and lower level councils were permitted to put forward nominations for the office of chief meant that in practice they had the opportunity of exercising power in a significant quarter. Finally, although the Ordinance did not give the councils any defined responsibilities, it did give them the right to discuss a wide variety of matters (such as communal labour or tax evasion) that fell within the chiefs' jurisdiction and which affected the mass of the rural population.

The African local governments of 1949 were in no sense autonomous local government bodies. The Uganda government had not, in fact, responded very enthusiastically to Colonial Office policy on the development of local government outlined in the Secretary of State's despatch of 1947.[10] That despatch had enunciated the Secretary of State's belief that the key to success in political, social, and economic advancement lay 'in the development of an efficient and democratic system of local government'. The Uganda Governor, Sir John Hall, proposed the establishment of provincial councils to counter the imbalance between Buganda and the other Provinces that even then exercised the official mind. But he did not take steps to give any genuine powers to the councils that his officers took so much trouble to establish. This had to await his successor, Sir Andrew Cohen, who speeded up an inquiry into the local governments carried out in 1953 by C. A. G. Wallis from the Colonial Office. Wallis' Report then provided the basis for significant changes under the District Councils (District Administrations) Ordinance of 1955.[11]

The 1955 Ordinance provided for enlarged and more representative district councils which should be responsible for the district's affairs. The intention behind the Ordinance was 'that in regard to district affairs the District Council should run them and the chiefs should be their executive officers'.[12] The *District Council*, consisting of *ex officio*, elected, and nominated members, became the *District Administration*. Any district council that wished could under the Ordinance introduce an elected majority and an elected unofficial chairman. Each district council would in future elect its own committees, the most important of which (besides the finance committee) was an appointments committee responsible for staff matters including the appointment, promotion, and dismissal of all senior officers including chiefs. The chiefs would become the servants of the district administration. Under the old African Authority Ordinance,[13] however, which was retained, they also remained responsible to the Governor for the maintenance of law and order. They were thus more obviously than in the past responsible to two different authorities. The district administrations' functions were considerably enlarged, with the devolution upon them of responsibility for additional services.

In 1955 therefore Uganda took a long step towards the establishment of representative local government, and the district councils assumed a much more significant role in the administration of the district. The District Councils (District Administration) Ordinance was, however, permissive and each council was left to decide how much of it to adopt. Consequently no two councils developed in the same way, and until 1962 no two councils followed the same rules. Three districts, Busoga, Toro, and Bukedi, refused to adopt the 1955 Ordinance at all, remaining under the 1949 African Local Government regulations. The composition and structure of the other councils, all of which adopted the new Ordinance, varied considerably. Some immediately introduced direct elections, some did not; some had an official, some an unofficial majority. The committee system varied between councils. The extent of the services performed was uneven. The pattern of local government between 1955 and 1962 was not therefore entirely uniform throughout the country. In all cases, however, it became more important and it enhanced the political status of the district.

The ability of the new district administration to handle the affairs of their districts also varied considerably. One difficulty that all encountered arose out of local political interest in the control and appointment of staff, which led to considerable conflict over such appointments. An extreme case occurred in Teso District, where political tensions in the council and appointments committee had by 1958 become so critical that the management of the district was brought to a halt and a Commission appointed to enquire into the district administration's conduct of its affairs recommended, *inter alia*, that the control of appointments of staff should be returned to the central government.[14] This was a view that the latter had held for some time, having already decided that the transfer of control of staff had been a mistake. Under amending legislation passed in 1958 the appointments committees were therefore replaced by appointments boards consisting of members appointed by the Governor from names submitted by each council. The Governor in Council made Regulations, uniform throughout the Protectorate, for appointments, promotions, and other staff matters.[15]

The Teso situation demonstrated how the infusion of factional politics into local government could adversely affect its functioning. Notwithstanding such problems, by the late 1950s most district administrations were bodies of considerable size and standing, performing a wide range of functions that provided important services for the districts. Most had introduced a graduated tax that formed the basis of their revenue. Most were spending considerable sums on basic services, including education, health, and roads—in a number of cases beyond their resources. All were institutions of considerable significance and their administration affected the daily life of the rural population to a very large extent. This was the level of government that was most significant for the vast majority of the people and most relevant to their daily lives.

A major review of local government institutions, carried out in connection with the constitutional settlement preceding independence, consolidated and enlarged these local administrations. It brought all local government under the same regulations, based on new legislation, the Local Administration Ordinance 1962 and the Administration (Western Kingdoms and Busoga) Act 1963. A *Local Administration* would in future consist of either a ruler, ministers, and a council; or a constitutional head and council; or a chief executive officer and council. All would enjoy similar authority and responsibilities. Each council had a chairman elected by secret ballot, who did not necessarily have to be an elected councillor but who could not be employed by the district administration. A Local Government Service Commission (later restyled the Regional Service Commission) would appoint a local service commission or appointments board for every administration, which would be responsible for appointments. While each council was left to decide on its actual composition, all had to meet the general requirement that nine-tenths of the members must be directly elected, on the same franchise as that used for national elec· tions. All councils (with the exception of Karamojo) assumed similar responsibilities for services which were now more clearly defined. The introduction of a political executive and a constitutional head, described earlier, gave the districts a substantial enlargement of status.

The considerable local interest shown in these successive changes during the 1950s demonstrated that local government institutions at the district level had acquired political significance for the local

public. When C. A. G. Wallis toured the country in 1953 he dis-
covered consistent opposition from chiefs and other district leaders
to the suggestion that the word 'government' should be removed
from the title of the proposed district administrations.[16] The Protectorate government delayed the passage of the local government
legislation based on his report from November 1953 until January
1955 because of the insistence of the African members of the Legislative Council that it should be referred to the districts for their
comment. As a result, during 1954 a Committee of the Legislative
Council, including virtually all the African elected members, under
the chairmanship of the Attorney-General, Mr Dreschfield, toured all
districts to receive public views on the Bill. In one district after
another local leaders argued for greater powers for their 'African
Local Governments'. As a result of the enquiry the Bill was in fact
modified in favour of the districts. In addition the title of the Bill
was changed to overcome fears that the district councils would not
receive executive powers; it was at that stage that the councils won
the control over appointments that was subsequently withdrawn.[17]

Most of the African members of the Legislative Council were
also drawn into these discussions in 1954 and 1955, spending a considerable time debating them both at the district enquiries and in
the Legislative Council. In 1958 they strongly objected to the changes
in the appointments committees, and at all times they were quick to
criticize any other proposed changes that suggested infringement of
district councils' rights. This contributed to the characteristic local
focus of politics until the latter part of the decade.

It has been argued that one of the reasons for the slow emergence
of political parties in Uganda was that politics at the district level—
within these developing local government institutions—were suffi-
ciently satisfying in themselves to politically-minded Africans, and
that as a consequence there was less desire on their part to participate
in 'nationalist' politics and the new political parties.[18] When we look
more closely at political activity at district level in the districts outside
Buganda during the 1950s, however, what emerges is more complicated than this. In fact, political activity at the district level during that
period was itself largely nationalist in orientation. It was focused on
the district largely because there were institutions at that level within
which the colonial authority could be challenged. The local authorities
offered the opportunity of office and patronage and power, and the
district councils also developed faster than the Legislative Council
so far as representation was concerned. Opportunities for election
to political office were thus available at district level before they were
at the centre. The district council as a result became an important

political arena for nationally-orientated local leaders. And those leaders in turn provided the links through which the African leadership at the centre could build the support it needed to confront the Protectorate government.

The provincial administration embarked enthusiastically on the extension of the council system to northern Uganda in the 1940s, seeing it as a means of combining old and new political influences. The then Provincial Commissioner for the province, J. W. Steil, claimed in 1947 that

the system of local, county and district councils . . . is the most suitable form of government which has yet been devised for peoples whose social structure stresses the clan relationship to the exclusion of the individual. The head of the clan is responsible for the welfare of the clan and representation from among the clan heads ensures that the interests of the clans will not be ignored, and that the traditional authorities of the elders will be given due weight in the tribal council. On the other hand the voice of the younger generation . . . is represented by the leaders of the young men in the Local Councils and by the nominated members of all the Councils. The balance between 'conservatism' and 'reform' is preserved.[19]

Thus he, like many other officials of his day, saw the local councils as the system through which representation would be built up, and local grievances and interests articulated, within the framework of the existing colonial system. The remainder of this essay will be concerned with the manner in which this affected the growth of parties and politics in the two northern districts of Acholi and Lango, and the pattern of politics that consequently emerged.

# 4

## POLITICS IN LANGO DISTRICT 1945–1962

Lango District is the smallest of the Northern Province districts, although the Lango people form the largest single ethnic group in that region. By the early 1950s its population density was as great as that of West Nile and it had the highest rate of increase. This fairly dense population was generally evenly distributed over the flat well-watered savannah-like country, except in the Kwania-Maruzi peninsula (which tsetse fly kept sparsely populated) and in Erute county around Lira, the district headquarters, which was itself a small but growing township of under 2,000. As has already been pointed out, cotton and cattle made Lango the most prosperous district in the province. There was more money going into the district to growers from exports than into either Acholi or West Nile.

Before the British occupation Lango lacked a strong central political system. In the absence of centralized political institutions the village and clan had been the two most important groups for the individual, the village of up to a hundred households being primarily an economic and defensive unit and the clan, while considerably larger than the village, still a relatively small group. The main characteristics of political organization were, first, its small scale, and, second, the importance of individual leadership within the system. Each village had a leader, called a chief (*jago*) whose most important function was leadership in war and who is consequently often described as a 'war leader'. He also settled disputes within the group and between clans in his neighbourhood. A *jago* who by his prowess emerged as a dominant leader in the neighbourhood, and who proved an outstanding military leader, became a *rwot*, or more powerful leader, although still not with the kind of authority as the *rwot* in the Acholi system. Although the *rwodi* were primarily military leaders, they also settled inter-clan quarrels within their sphere of influence and maintained a balance between group interests. Because they were rivals, there was considerable inter-clan strife. The leadership of *rwodi* depended largely on personality and success, and their domains were for the most part small, nor did there seem any general tendency for larger political units to emerge. There were six major clans or groupings but these were dispersed and it is doubtful whether

clan was politically important in the pre-colonial period. More
significant were the *etogo* groups, the four groups that linked different
clans together for ritual and social purposes, and which appear to
have been territorial. Through these *etogo*, described as interlineage
ceremonial organizations, there was an extensive interlocking of clan
groups, which held the Lango together in the larger tribe without
any central authority. The Lango political system was thus a loose
and simple one, which however allowed an individual considerable
scope to rise to prominence by personal merits and power. Natural
leadership was thus important.

The introduction of British rule imposed on the Langi an administrative system and a centralized control they had not previously
known. British administration put an end to the pre-colonial warfare;
it also created a new class of chiefs. Some of the Langi appointed
by the British as chiefs in the early years, taking over from the original
Ganda agents, were prominent local leaders before the British advance.
Others were sons of such leaders, as were Yakobo Adoko and Isaya
Ogwangujji, who were the dominant county chiefs in the late 1940s
and early 1950s. The authority they wielded and the role they
performed was however very different from their 'war leader' fore-
bears.

Clan did not appear seriously to divide the Langi nor were there any
other deep divisions based on religion or economic class. It remained a
very obviously egalitarian society, with the exception of the chiefly
families. Administrators in Lango District in the late 1940s nevertheless
reported a 'real and lively interest' in local affairs, greater than in the
other Northern Province districts. The most politically active group
since the end of the Second World War had been the county chiefs,
who were men of considerable standing and power within the district.
To what extent men of this group at this time enjoyed any claim to
traditional legitimacy it is difficult to say, in the light of existing knowledge of pre-colonial structures in Lango. Since Lango leaders had in the
past been first and foremost war leaders, with no administrative
authority and no hereditary succession, the British had found no chiefly
system they could exploit for administrative purposes. In introducing
into Lango a new administrative structure, based on the Ganda model,
they had obviously looked in the early years for outstanding men in the
community. But they appointed their agents on merit and chiefs in
Lango were from the outset 'appointed' agents who had no recognized
traditional authority.[1] As a group then these men did not enjoy their
position by virtue of any pre-colonial legitimacy, although some might
have claimed this.

In experience and qualifications the county chiefs of the late 1940s differed a good deal. Rwot Ogwangujji, the senior chief, was illiterate. He had first been appointed a chief in 1913, a county chief in 1917, and was finally to retire in 1955. Rwot Yakobo Adoko, the other most senior chief, who claimed a relationship with a pre-colonial leader and was in the late 1940s the dominant figure in the Lango native administration, had also been one of the first Langi to be made a chief, having succeeded his father as a sub-county chief in 1917. Rwot Eria Olet, Ogwangujji's half-brother, had on the other hand been the first Lango boy to go south to school, to Buddo College in Buganda, in the 1920s. He had become a chief in 1934.[2]

Whatever their experience or education the county chiefs were a superior class economically, and economic status as well as administrative authority made them a powerful group. There was a good deal of jockeying for power among them, and considerable man-oeuvring for personal dominance within the native administration and the district. The provincial administration saw this rivalry and competition as a reflection of clan rivalries but the available evidence suggests that the competition was more within the small group of dominant families, and was focused primarily on Rwot Yakobo Adoko and Rwot Ogwangujji, each of whom wished to dominate the Lango system, and their respective families.

In the 1940s at the time of the introduction into Lango of the new council system the county chiefs campaigned for increased powers for the district, from which they would themselves have benefited considerably. This move began in 1944 when the members asked the provincial administration to reorganize the district council. Their proposals included, first, the appointment of one of the county chiefs as secretary-general of the native administration (as in Teso) to deal with district affairs, with the assistance of a standing committee and the district council; and, second, the appointment of a second county chief as Lango native administration President of the court, to deal with all appeals from the counties. Both of these, it was suggested, should be elected by the council itself every three years. It was also proposed that a Lango man should be appointed to the new post of treasurer of the native administration and Yakobo Omonya, also half-brother to Ogwangujji who had been to Makerere in the 1930s and who was at the time head clerk in the District Commissioner's office in Arua, was proposed as a suitable candidate who should be sent to Entebbe for training. A second Lango man was also proposed as assistant treasurer. The council wished to appoint a standing committee, consisting of two county chiefs, three sub-county chiefs and four other members of the council; and a finance committee, which would include unofficials, and which would assume responsibility for drafting the annual estimates (hitherto drawn up by the District Commissioner).[3]

All this implied a considerable increase of power for the county chiefs (who dominated the district council at that stage) and for the status of the district. The immediate influence was almost certainly that of Teso, where there had been a recent expansion in the native administration with the appointment of a new official, a secretary-general.[4] Acholi District also raised the same question at this time, hoping for the appointment of a secretary-general comparable to the Teso post. Events in Gulu influenced the Lango council petition and the demonstration effect of Buganda must also be taken into effect. What the Lango chiefs wanted was a *district* leader rather like the Kabaka who would have increased powers within the district, and who would provide them with a spokesman at the centre, and they wanted this office for one of themselves.

The Protectorate government agreed on the need to enlarge the personnel and reorganize the headquarters of the district council. Although it was many months before any conclusions were reached on the chiefs' proposals, most of them in somewhat modified form were therefore accepted. Mr Omonya was sent to Entebbe for training and subsequently became district cashier.[5] A standing committee of the Lango District Council was established, although with the District Commissioner as chairman, and not (as the council had proposed) a secretary-general.

What the Protectorate government rejected was the proposal for a secretary-general with the status and power envisaged by the county chiefs. They believed there was an urgent need for an official at the native administration headquarters to coordinate the work of the chiefs, the provincial administration, and the Lango district council but they saw him as a rather low-ranking official, somewhat like a junior secretary. The county chiefs for their part envisaged the post of secretary-general as one with considerable powers, not simply of coordination, and they argued with the provincial administration about the appointment for two years. It was during this time that they put forward the idea of a *won nyaci* or paramount chief for the district.[6] The provincial administration categorically rejected the proposal for two reasons. In the first place they had encountered considerable difficulties in Busoga as a result of the recognition of one of the *saza* (county) chiefs there as Kyabazinga, or leader of the district, and were determined not to have a repetition of that experience.[7] The *won nyaci* appeared to them exactly the same kind of paramount. In the second place they considered that any kind of paramount chief was alien to Lango institutions. They believed the stimulus behind the campaign came from one faction among the county chiefs, supported by Rwot Yakobo Adoko, in an attempt to entrench the latter (and therefore his family and clan) in a dominant political position, and they denounced it as clan rivalry.

It is difficult to believe that clan would have been the source of such rivalry, since clans in Lango are numerous, widely dispersed, and had not enjoyed in the pre-colonial period any great political significance. The six major clan groupings into which the Langi were divided are territorially very dispersed. Thus the earlier suggestion that the rivalries were based on family groupings seems the more likely explanation of the factionalism that emerged over the *won nyaci* issue. Yakobo Adoko's own behaviour at the time suggested that his ambitions lay in that direction and the group of county chiefs was clearly divided over who should occupy the office if it was established.[8] Whatever the foundation of the district cleavages at that time, the fundamental significance of the *won nyaci* campaign lay however in another direction: the county chiefs wanted more power and they were asserting themselves against the provincial administration for control of the district. At the same time they faced some opposition from younger men in the district who had established the Young Lango Association in 1944, and who also wanted a greater share in district affairs and in the native administration.[9]

The county chiefs failed to achieve their objective when the district council refused to make an appointment to the comparatively junior post of secretary, to which the provincial administration had agreed, whereupon the District Commissioner proceeded to make the appointment himself. The deadlock was resolved finally in 1948, when the latter removed the dissident element from the standing committee, which was then persuaded to confirm the appointment.[10]

The district council returned to the question of a *won nyaci* in 1950 when the 1949 Ordinance made further local reorganization necessary. By then the provincial administration, although still firmly opposed to the idea of a paramount chief, had found that the secretary appointed to the native administration provided inadequate liaison with the county chiefs. The recently established African local government also seemed to require a more senior official. The district council proposed to upgrade the post of chairman of the district council (held by a county chief), who would be given certain executive powers, and called the *won nyaci*. The provincial administration rejected this suggestion. But they agreed to the title *rwot adwong* for an official, elected by the district council from among the county chiefs, who would be both chairman of the council and senior executive officer of the Lango (African) local government.[11] Rwot Ogwangujji was appointed by the District Commissioner as the first holder of this office. When he retired in 1952 he was succeeded by Yakobo Adoko, elected by the council.

One might almost ask 'what's in a name?' since the *rwot adwong* enjoyed to a large extent the position and authority which the chiefs had earlier hoped to endow on a *won nyaci*: he was chairman of the district council, with executive powers, in charge of the Lango local government. What he did not have, however, was political power over the district. That continued to lie with the District Commissioner.

It is difficult to assess whether the *won nyaci* campaign had popular backing among the rural population in Lango in the 1940s. The provincial administration believed that it did.[12] The question of popular support is, however, of less relevance to the pattern of political activity in these years than the fact that the conflict was over political control, between politically active Lango men and the Protectorate government, at the district level. The battle had been started by the county chiefs. Later it would be taken over by others in the district who represented different political interests but desired the same end.

While the county chiefs sought power in the Lango local government, popular interest had developed in the subordinate councils introduced between 1944 and 1947. The composition of these councils, which followed the general pattern outlined above, is of some significance. In Lango the village (*pacho*) council consisted of the *pacho* chief as chairman, ten clan heads, and twenty peasants, all elected by acclamation by the male adults of the village.[13] Two clan heads and three elected members were selected by that council to sit on the next higher council, the sub-county (*jago*) council, which consisted altogether of the sub-county chief as chairman, two parish chiefs (*jan jegi*), six village chiefs, one per village, two 'prominent citizens' nominated by the rest of the council, twelve clan heads, two for each village, and eighteen other members, three from each village. This council in turn sent forward one official and two elected members to the county council, chaired by the county chief. Finally at the top of the pyramid was the Lango District Council, a large body of over eighty members, including all the county chiefs and seventeen sub-county chiefs, the native administration secretary and cashier, ten members nominated by the district council, ten more nominated by the District Commissioner, and thirty-seven elected members, one from each sub-county. There was therefore a representative element in all councils throughout the district.[14]

These councils had no executive powers, as was true generally of the councils at that time. They were intended as forums for discussion on local affairs at each administrative level, where unofficials as well as chiefs would participate. Under the Standing Orders drawn up by the Lango Native District Council in October 1946, the lower councils were therefore given the right to discuss a wide range of matters that concerned the district as a whole. The village council was permitted to make recommendations to the sub-county council on local administrative matters such as grazing, soil cultivation, water supplies and education. The sub-county council was required to submit estimates and make recommendations to the county council for the maintenance of the chief's headquarters and for local services such as roads, pumps, and dams. The county council considered the estimates from the sub-county councils and in turn submitted estimates to the finance committee of the district council. The district council could discuss any matter concerning the district and pass resolutions on those matters, although these were subject to the Provincial Commissioner's approval. Any member could raise any subject concerning Lango District, although no decision could be reached before it had been referred to the standing committee (of which the District Commissioner was chairman). In theory, therefore, nothing was excluded from public discussion at one or other administrative level. What the councils lacked was the power to implement their decisions.[15]

As in other districts the councils had an important role to play as arbiters in purely local affairs. They also enjoyed in common with other councils one other power which was of particular importance: they had the right to put forward nominations for chiefs, although the final appointment remained the responsibility of the Governor. Under the new Council Rules of 1946 the village council could make recommendations to the sub-county council on the appointment of the village chief who, as a local appointment, was rarely moved from his village. Similarly, the sub-county council could make recommendations to the county council on appointments to any vacancies in the sub-county; and the county council put up recommendations to the standing committee of the district council on appointments to county and sub-county chiefs. The district council then voted on two or three names to be put forward to the District Commissioner by the standing committee to fill vacancies as county or sub-county chief, native administration secretary, and native administration cashier. There was no legal basis for this. Recommendations were subject to the District Commissioner's approval and could be overruled. The District Commissioner was moreover chairman of the standing committee. Nevertheless, it was of considerable significance, given the role of the chief in the district, that the councils should be permitted to participate in his selection, and this significance was appreciated in the district by men prepared to challenge the authority of both provincial and native administration.[16] Moreover, the attitude of the chief was bound to be affected by the knowledge that his appointment could be the subject of discussion in the council of his own administrative area.

It was these councils, and particularly the village councils (of which there were 230 in the district by 1953) which attracted public attention. Although they had no executive functions, they nevertheless provided an opportunity for the expression of views. Administrative officers on tour visited these regularly and encouraged them, particularly in the early stages, to discuss local affairs and to put forward resolutions to the higher council; they also tried to ensure that higher councils attended to these resolutions quickly to ensure the continuation of public interest. It is impossible to assess accurately how extensive or sustained was this popular participation over the whole district. In some places councils met weekly regardless of whether or not there was business to discuss. Such enthusiasm was not generated in all councils. But two points emerge from the touring reports of administrative officers: first an impression of lively discussions on local affairs in some councils in every county; and second the development of the council as a focus for political debate by a politically active minority.[17] It was not long, moreover, before some members of the lower level councils began to ask for executive powers. By 1957 the elected members on the district council were demanding greater powers for the district council as opposed to the native administration. The unofficials wanted to exercise the authority enjoyed by the chiefs.[18]

By the time this challenge emerged the character of unofficial representation on the district council had changed. There had of course been unofficials in the Lango native council since 1938. Until 1944 they had been nominated by the District Commissioner after consultation with the chiefs; they had been drawn from the small educated group in the district, particularly the teachers. The Young Lango Association, which had been formed in 1937 by a small group of teachers and county chiefs to promote educational opportunities in the district, had requested and been given a representative on the council. Jaholyn Odyek, who was Principal of the Aler Farm School just outside Lira, had been appointed.[19] Mr Odyek remained a member of the council in the 1940s, along with T. K. Otim, an assistant agricultural officer, E. O. Olyech, then (1946) a clerk in the native administration office, and Y. W. Apenyo, a court clerk. The two missions, the Roman Catholics at Ngetta and the native Anglican Church at

Boroboro, each also had a representative (nominated in this case by the District Commissioner).

This group of unofficials, representing the educated element in the community, had all been anxious to see the district progress. They had, however, accepted the existing administrative structure as the basis for development, although they had been critical of the chiefs and sought reforms in the native administration.[20] They had been involved in the *won nyaci* campaign, some of them supporting the chiefs' demands. This is not perhaps surprising, since the chiefs at that time exercised considerable influence over the selection of the unofficials.

The introduction of indirect elections in the late 1940s brought a new kind of person on to the council. It became possible for the ordinary villager, farmer, or trader to become a member. In 1948 the District Commissioner described it as filled 'with the most talkative peasants' and thought that 'a lot has been sacrificed to the democratic principle'.[21] These new men were more representative of the rural population, and regarded themselves as representing the district populace. They were less deferential, less wealthy, more critical, and generally more militant than the more educated unofficials.[22] They raised new kinds of grievances from the rural areas which had not hitherto been discussed by the district council. At the meeting of April 1950, for example, elected members criticized the working of the cotton marketing system and the behaviour of European administrative officers on tour.[23] They also questioned the status of the native administration, as compared with the African local government, and demanded more authority for the district council. After the meeting of October 1951 they wrote to the Governor to complain that resolutions passed in the council were ignored by the provincial administration, and asked whether this was 'training for democracy or dictatorship system of government'.[24] They challenged the District Commissioner when he ignored the provision which gave them the right to vote on elections of chiefs. Thus in 1951 when the new post of *rwot adwong* was established and the District Commissioner appointed Rwot Ogwangujji, then the most senior county chief, without any consultation with the council, the unofficial members (and on this occasion also the other county chiefs) took strong exception to the decision on the grounds both that their right to choose the official had been ignored and that Ogwangujji was not a suitable candidate. At the council meeting of November 1952 they put forward a request (refused by C. Powell-Cotton, then District Commissioner) that unofficial members should be made members of the district team.[25] At the same meeting one of the newly elected members,

Yokosafati Engur, also proposed a strict educational test for chiefs of a standard that few of the chiefs then holding office could have passed. By the end of 1952 therefore, the elected members of the Lango district council had demonstrated their intention of challenging the dominant position of the officials and chiefs on the African local government bodies. It is not surprising, therefore, that Yakobo Adoko, when he later recalled these years, said of the councils: 'these have spoilt the work and life of the chiefs'.[26]

There was an additional reason why after 1952 the district council received increased attention from those anxious to assume political influence: from that time onwards Lango, in company with all other districts, was drawn into the discussions about proposed political and constitutional changes for Uganda as a whole. Wallis' local government enquiry in 1952 was the first of a succession of official government commissions and committees, all of which consulted each district council on various constitutional and administrative issues raised by the Protectorate government. The draft proposals for local government legislation, based upon the Wallis Report of 1953, were discussed twice in 1954 at district level: first with the standing committees by a Protectorate government official who visited each district in turn, and then by a Committee of Members of the Legislative Council who toured the country under the chairmanship of the Attorney-General, Ralph Dreschfield, interviewing not only the standing committee but other councillors as well.[27] When the question of direct elections to the Legislative Council was raised in 1956, a Protectorate official visited each district council to elicit their views for a Legislative Council committee then sitting in Kampala.[28] In 1959 the Wild Committee held meetings with members of all district councils on the subject of constitutional development. In 1961 the Munster Commission, set up by the Secretary of State to enquire into the question of relations between the districts and the central government in an independent Uganda, visited each district and each district council. The district council therefore occupied an influential position as the body which put forward district views on a variety of major issues that would affect not only the district but also the Protectorate in the future. Local government officials (the secretaries-general and council chairmen), moreover, met on a number of occasions between 1958 and 1962 to discuss constitutional and political affairs and their views were listened to by the Protectorate government. Not surprisingly, therefore, there was a contest between the different interests in the district for control of the council, and therefore of the views put forward.

This contest began as one between the county chiefs and the new group of indirectly elected members. Its intensity in the early 1950s should not be exaggerated. At that time the unofficials were few in number. They had no common organization and little bargaining power. It is doubtful whether their activities generated a strong popular response in the district as a whole. In those years, Lango, like the rest of the Northern Province, was not in a state of political ferment. Nevertheless, the debate in the district council indicated the emergence of a new element in district politics, and the expansion of the number of participants in the local political arena.

It was at that point that the newly formed Uganda National Congress (UNC), the first modern political party to be established in Uganda, appeared in Lango District. The UNC, formed in Kampala in March 1952, set up a branch in Lango at the end of the same year, after a visit to Lira by the party's founders, I. K. Musazi and Abu Mayanja. The first branch chairman was Yokosafati Engur, who had been the leader of the Lango branch of the Uganda African Farmers' Federation established in 1951. Local support for the new party grew originally out of support given to the Federation. The UNC branch was launched at a time when government policy on cotton prices and marketing was being questioned, and Musazi's economic platform aroused some local response. It was also a time when the Langi were becoming more self-assertive, seeking to establish an independent identity instead of being looked at simply as part of the north. (They objected, for example, to the language policy of the period, which generally assumed Acholi to be the common language for the two districts.) Musazi's talk of self-government appealed to teachers and other educated members of the community as well as to the peasants. The Lira meeting at which the branch was launched was well attended by small farmers, subsistence cultivators, shopkeepers, traders, and some teachers. One man who was present at the meeting, remembering it ten years later—perhaps in too glowing terms—spoke of it as 'just a miracle. Everyone was given a chance to speak on the subject of his interest.' These subjects included education, language, and cotton prices.[29]

A meeting in Lira late in 1952 appointed a local committee of eight to assist Engur to organize the party throughout the district and to establish local contacts at county and lower levels. That group then toured the district and appointed a local man in each county as a party agent, whose responsibility was to build up support within the county. Although the committee had a room in Lira township which they used as an office, the branch had very little formal organization either at its headquarters or in the villages. Nor did it build up a large subscription-paying membership although people did contribute to party funds. Its organization and style of politics was essentially informal, based on personal links between Engur and the other committee members and their county and village supporters, with whom they would talk about the party and take up local issues. There was a good deal of this kind of informal activity in 1953. The committee also had several meetings with the Provincial or District Commissioner at which they raised local grievances.

The founder members of the Lango UNC were men of varying educational and other backgrounds but they were all local men who had been previously interested in Lango African local government politics. Some of them were already unofficial members of the district council. Most had belonged to the Young Lango Association. Three of them, Engur, the chairman, Ben Otim, and Semei Ngwenge, had been local leaders of Musazi's Federation of African Farmers. Engur (who was Rwot Yokobo Adoko's nephew) had had secondary school education and had worked first as a District Commissioner's interpreter and then (after some training) as a medical dresser. That employment had taken him outside the district to Kigezi and Kampala (where he had worked in Mulago hospital) before he was transferred back to Lira. During his time in Kampala he had come into contact with Musazi and the new political ideas then being generated in Buganda. In June 1951, faced with the possibility of a transfer out of the district, he had resigned to become a 'full-time politician' and taken up work for the Federation of Farmers. At the time of the formation of UNC in Lango, therefore, he was the most important link between the district and politically active men further south.[30]

Of the others, Ben Otim had been to Gulu High School in the early 1940s and had then worked with the local (military) rehabilitation/welfare officer in Lira. In 1948 he became secretary of the Lango Shopkeepers' Cooperative Society which had tried, unsuccessfully, to provide wholesale facilities for African traders to enable them to break into the local retail trade. Ngwenge was a small trader with only primary education, who had become President of the Shopkeepers' Cooperative. A fourth man, Olyech, who had been on the district council since the late 1940s but whose position within the branch is much more difficult to determine, had been a clerk in the Lango local government and then a storekeeper. He was the only member of the group who had been in the army, having travelled as far as Nairobi in the King's African Rifles. These men became full-time politicians. They received no regular income from the party but each had his plot and a family to cultivate it. Ngwenge had his small shop. All could count on hospitality when they travelled through the district.

Their agents at county level were for the most part small farmers or small traders; one or two were primary schoolteachers. With a few exceptions, they had had only primary education. Others associated with the UNC in these early years, either in the Lira committee or at county or village levels, were men of similar background: primary schoolteachers, farmers, and traders. Most of them were Protestants. None occupied an important official position in the district and, with the exception of Engur, none was related to the elite of county chiefs and their families. The only way in which they might be distinguished from other Langi was in so far as some of them had been associated with the politically active section of the community who, in the late 1940s and early 1950s, had been seeking greater power for the unofficials within the council system. They had also been associated with attempts to improve the position of the Lango, such as the formation of the Shopkeepers' Cooperative.

Although teachers did not assume any public role in the new party because their terms of service precluded them from political affiliation, many local schoolmasters felt considerable sympathy for the UNC. This was especially true of native Anglican church teachers and schoolmasters, including those at Boroboro, the central Anglican mission centre outside Lira. The party also enjoyed a good deal of covert support from NAC churchmen who, having seen the growth of African participation in the church in the Eastern Province, wanted a similar (enlarged) role for themselves in the church in Lango. Events suggested that the branch also enjoyed the support of several chiefs. Some of the party's agents and supporters might in some ways be considered men of substance in a community of peasant farmers. Teachers of any category occupied a position of importance in the community. Traders and shopkeepers, even if their business was small, had moved beyond the farming community. All would have had opportunities for contact and communication, through their trading activities and shops, and for raising political issues. Thus Ngwenge's shop was a focal point for discussion at which he and others would no doubt have raised party issues and discussed what took place in the councils. He and other traders must also have gone to the markets which had sprung up throughout the countryside in the 1940s, and where a crowd would congregate, 'cattle are slaughtered for sale, food and gossip exchanged, beer is drunk and a good time had by all'. At such market gatherings it is reasonable to assume politics were discussed and political education took place. The 'talkative' councillors would also, it may be assumed, have been prominent on such occasions, and have drawn around them then and at other times groups of kinsmen, clansmen, and village associates whose political education they would take in hand. These councillors, who provided the lower political echelons below the district and county level agents, helped to extend the new politics of the district, and to draw people into it. Given the characteristic Lango emphasis on achievement and individual leadership, it is possible they won their positions by virtue of being to some extent men of substance in the community. On the other hand all the (remembered) accounts of these men emphasize not their property, but rather their ability to articulate local grievances against the men of substance, the chiefs.

The Lango UNC was a district branch of a national party with its headquarters in Kampala. Engur, as branch chairman, went to Kampala for party meetings and there were other intermittent contacts between UNC headquarters and the branch. Engur also joined the UNC delegation that went to England in 1955 to petition the Secretary of State for the Kabaka's return. Party leaders in Kampala failed, however, to establish an effective central organization, with the result that the Lango branch was scarcely controlled from the centre. Communication in the following four or five years between its leaders and UNC groups in other districts was also limited. There was some communication with the Acholi branch of the party, especially in the Kitgum area. Otherwise there was only a limited amount of inter-district visiting. After Milton Obote became Lango's representative in the Legislative Council in March 1958, he became an important link between district and centre. But for the most part the Lango UNC developed up to 1960 as an autonomous unit.

It is necessary to remember this relative autonomy in looking at the political objectives that the branch took up in the following few years and the tactics adopted to achieve them. It is also important to bear in mind the absence of serious economic or social grievances within the Lango community in these same years. When Musazi first visited the district there existed local discontent over the price of cotton and the arrangements for the marketing of cash crops but soon after his visit crop prices improved and the Protectorate government considerably altered its overall policy on prices and marketing. There was a good deal of money coming into the district. There were consequently no major economic grievances in the early 1950s when the Lango UNC set out to arouse support for its policy of political change and self-government, but only 'muted discontent' common throughout the province.

From the outset the Lango UNC leaders were fighting the chiefs for the local leadership in the district. In doing so they adopted three different but related lines of action: they held public rallies in Lira; they tried to establish their right as an organization to meet the District Commissioner as the legitimate spokesmen for the Lango people as a whole; and they set out to obtain control of the local council system.

At their public meetings held in Lira Engur and other speakers put forward what can be described as typical nationalist demands for political change in Uganda's central government institutions. They raised and publicized the major national political issues of the 1950s, one being government policy on multi-racialism, particularly the appointment (in 1955) of an Asian Minister to the Executive Council. At meetings in December 1954 and May 1955 they rejected the principle of multi-racial government and in 1955 demanded an African parliament for Uganda.[31] A second issue was the existing method of African representation in the Legislative Council, because it meant that many members were local government officials. Third, in October 1956 (by which time the question of national elections had been raised), and on other occasions, they demanded direct elections on a common roll in 1957 for all Members of the Legislative Council and explicitly opposed special treatment for Buganda. Fourth, in October 1957, a UNC meeting in Lira supported the African Legislative Council Members' opposition to the proposals for special representation for the minority communities and called upon 'the Lukiko, Rukuratos, Eishengyero, and all African District Councils to convene a National Assembly of members from their councils to assume responsibility for the direction of our national affairs and thereby supersede the Legislative Council'. The UNC platform at the party's public rallies in the bus park in Lira was therefore typically nationalist.

Public meetings were neither frequent nor regular. Attendance probably varied a good deal but seems unlikely on any occasion to have exceeded five hundred. Nevertheless, such meetings were one method by which the branch broadcast its programme and made a bid for political leadership in the district. The UNC at the national level failed in this period to produce a clearly enunciated policy or even a manifesto. In Buganda the party was drawn into Ganda tribal conflicts which lost it its nationalist image. But the Lango branch of the party was at the same time independently making the broad nationalist demands common in every colonial territory at this stage of its development.

Local district issues were also discussed at these rallies. In June 1953 the branch organized a demonstration for the return of Lango's 'lost counties', an area that had at an earlier date been transferred to Teso District. They also talked about the Lango-Acholi boundary disputes which were a source of local friction. Other local grievances that they took up concerned cotton prices and marketing arrangements; the domination of local trade by Indians; the abolition of hawkers' licences; the alleged injustice of local taxes; local tax assessment, which was considered to be unfairly carried out; a government experimental TB scheme which the UNC leaders alleged would endanger Lango land; forced labour (*ber lobo*, the chiefs' right to call out unpaid labour for a number of community efforts); and the Protectorate government's land proposals of 1955.[32]

Since there were no major economic grievances in the district in the mid-1950s, it is doubtful whether the UNC criticisms of cotton prices and marketing arrangements alone would have won them significant local support particularly after the reforms of 1952. The economic and commercial potential of the district was, as we have seen earlier, still unrealized in the mid-1950s. This relative economic backwardness had not, however, become an acute local grievance. The one issue on which the Langi felt strongly was the question of land.[33] They were inherently suspicious of any Protectorate action or proposal concerning land and the stand which the UNC took over the government's 1955 land proposals proved highly influential in winning over a large number of Langi to the UNC. It is therefore necessary to look more closely at this issue.

Land in Lango District, as elsewhere in the Protectorate outside Buganda, was still at that time held under customary land tenure. There remained a good deal of unoccupied land available for settlement but a rapidly increasing population was creating new pressures for the future. In 1955, following the recommendations of the East African Royal Commission, the Protectorate government published proposals which would have permitted the introduction of freehold tenure in all districts.[34] There was no question of the imposition of legislation: the proposals were published for general discussion only. The government hoped that they would be favourably received and that legislation might follow. To its surprise, however, the proposals provoked immediate and widespread hostility in all districts except Kigezi. When every district council, except Kigezi, rejected them the government gave up the reforms for the time being.

In Lango itself there was widespread suspicion of any change in land tenure. Administrative officers encountered coolness or hostility when they discussed the proposals with the lower councils during 1956. It was rumoured that they were a preliminary to alienating land to Kenya Europeans, a rumour that gained currency from the visit of a group of chiefs to Kenya to see the progress of land consolidation there. 'It is incredible,' the District Commissioner reported, 'to see that some people still believed it was a plot to settle Europeans.' This hostility also arose, however, out of fears of encroachment by other Africans as well as Europeans. Of his discussions with the

Kwania councils in February 1956, the Assistant District Commissioner reported, for example:

Generally speaking the people could not see that they had much to lose. The fear of the intention of Europeans and Asians was evident in the hostility to Government's nomination of members to the Land Tenure Boards, but a stronger and more general apprehension was that the new system would enable other African tribes to secure land rights in Lango.[35]

The matter might have rested there, for the provincial administration gave an assurance that the Regulations would be introduced in Lango only if the district council itself agreed to them. A discussion on the Regulations at the meeting of the council in February 1956 passed off without any serious difficulty. At this point, however, the UNC took up the issue. At a public meeting in Lira on 3 March 1956 it passed a resolution objecting to the proposals, which was sent to the Chief Secretary and the Minister for Lands, and which proposed that the title of 'Crown Lands' should be changed to 'Uganda African Indigenous Lands'.[36] At a subsequent meeting in August the party protested against the chiefs' visit to the Central Province of Kenya, which ought, they insisted, to have been discussed by the district council before it was organized by the administration. The party also challenged a quite separate proposal that had been made at that time, to introduce cooperative farming among small land-holders from the Lango African Local Government Farm School at Aler, on the grounds that this was an attempt to introduce individual land tenure without the public realizing it.[37] In the months that followed leaders held numerous small meetings in the villages at which they articulated the existing popular suspicion and opposition to the proposals. As a result, by the time Mr Mungwanya, the Protectorate Minister for Land Tenure, arrived to address the November district council meeting about the government's proposals, a good deal more public hostility had been aroused. A crowd gathered outside the council, burst into the meeting, which broke up in disorder, and several people were injured.[38]

This episode stimulated a good deal of popular sympathy and support for the UNC among the rural population as a whole and promoted its claim to leadership. The chiefs incurred more hostility as servants of the government that had introduced these proposals. Not the least advantage of the episode for the party leaders was the publicity they subsequently received when administrative officers in council meetings publicly castigated them for their behaviour and when Engur was jailed for his part in the proceedings. Jacobs, the District Commissioner, and his Assistants spent a good deal of time at council meetings throughout the district in the following months, condemning the UNC for its part in the November disturbances and for their opposition to the land proposals; this official condemnation increased rather than decreased support for the party. As a result the UNC gained in popularity and, if it continued to have few paid-up members, it acquired an increased number of followers and supporters. The November 1956 disturbances in Lira thus marked an important step forward for it.

During this episode the UNC leaders had concentrated their efforts less on large public rallies in Lira than on small meetings in the villages and on speaking at meetings of the lower level councils. This was generally true of their tactics during the mid-1950s: they used the councils as forums within which they made their bid for local leadership. Since there were in 1953 approximately two hundred and thirty village councils in Lango District, they generally offered a useful means of communication in the rural areas. Ironically, the District Commissioner had hoped, in 1953, when the party first appeared on the scene, that it would work through these councils; the politicians, however, soon went too fast for the officials.[39]

The geographical spread of UNC activity is difficult to assess. It would be a mistake to exaggerate the extent of popular participation in its activities between 1953 and 1955, and certainly not every part of the district was drawn into party activities. Nevertheless there was a significant number of councils in the district where the UNC influenced discussions and where the administrative officers could rely on finding a small group of men ready to challenge government policy and the authority of the chiefs. Much of this activity was in Erute county, which surrounded Lira township. In Amach division, for example, in November 1953, the Assistant District Commissioner reported a 'hard core of ten UNC here, mainly shopkeepers. They hold meetings towards Agwata. Two have been locked up for conspiracy to burn down the *Jago*'s house.'[40] Bar division which was reported in 1953 to be 'a UNC stronghold'[41] was still in 1955 regarded as an area where the party was a challenge to the chiefs. The sub-county chief of a third division reported in 1954 that people would not come forward to work for the Lango local government because of UNC pressures and the party's opposition to the system of unpaid labour.[42] At Awelo and Aputi in Kioga County, Aboki in Oyam, and Aduku and Chawente in Maruzi County, similarly there were groups of UNC supporters who challenged the leadership of the chiefs and demanded greater authority for the councils. Thus in each county there were pockets of UNC supporters who publicized the party and actively engaged the administration in debate on political issues.

In most cases there were local circumstances that made an area receptive to the UNC. On the one hand, Erute County was the most politically active part of the district because of the proximity of Lira township, the influence of Boroboro School and mission, and the closer links with general political developments that resulted. Engur and Olyech both came from villages close to Lira, and all UNC district leaders spent a good deal of time there. In Kioga County, on the other hand, the mixed tribal composition of the area made the Lango minority responsive to UNC ideas which appeared to offer them the opportunity for greater local influence.

Local sympathies for the new politicians generally increased, however, when the latter supported the people over local grievances. Land was the major issue but there were other grievances, including the system of unpaid labour invoked by the chiefs: the behaviour of chiefs and the presents demanded by them; the regulations for famine reserves; Protectorate policy on forest reserves; and the treatment of labour at the lakeside port at Kachung. These were all matters that affected the daily life of most Langi and influenced their relations with chiefs and administrative officers. By opposing the government over these issues on behalf of the people, UNC leaders gathered sympathy and support. Few Langi actually appear to have joined the UNC in these early years but many, the evidence suggests, became sympathetic to the party and its ideas. They began implicitly to accept the party claim to leadership against the chiefs, who had in the past imposed their will upon councils and the community. Thus the UNC acquired rural support based on resentment against colonial rule, which was none the less real because its expression had always been restrained. The party also acquired supporters in the district council: a handful at first, which increased with the 1956 council elections. These supporters actively campaigned in the council, as members of UNC, for greater powers to control the executive at district level.

It is not surprising that the UNC should focus attention on the district council, for in the early years it offered them an arena on which they could make themselves heard at a time when there was no opportunity for participation at the national level. For a number of reasons the UNC's Kampala headquarters had failed to establish a coordinated national party machine. The events of the Buganda crisis from 1953 to the end of 1955 made it all the more difficult for the party to function as a national body. National party leadership was at that time lacking.[43] Moreover, there were no direct elections to national institutions that the UNC could contest.

The district council however, acting as an electoral college, chose the Lango member of the Legislative Council. This in itself gave control of the district council an increased political importance. In addition, from 1953 to 1955, local government reform was under active discussion. The Lango UNC supporters not unnaturally therefore looked on the district council as a place where they might exert their influence. Among those who gave evidence to the Dreschfield Committee in Lira in 1954 were Engur, Akaa, Olyech, Ben Otim, and Anyek, all UNC activists. Their evidence to the Committee can be guessed at from their statements in the district council meetings and from the demands they made at public rallies in Lira. They wanted politicians—elected members—to control the district administration. This objective was summed up aptly in a resolution passed at a Lira rally in August 1955, when they demanded a new constitution for Lango District Council to provide for three political posts at its head: a *won nyaci*, to be chairman of the council; a treasurer, responsible for finance; and a secretary-general to coordinate the departments; all three to be 'freely and directly elected by the Lango people on the basis of adult universal suffrage'.[44] They wanted the executive powers enjoyed by the provincial administration and the native authority to be transferred to an elected council. This was a nationalist objective: the desire to take over from the colonial ruler; in this case, however, it led to a greater emphasis on the district than on the national arena. As the District Commissioner put it, they wanted 'a ministerial system' at district level. Whether or not, in taking up the demand for a *won nyaci* made earlier by the county chiefs, the party directly supported one faction's claim to office, they assumed it would mean the transfer of executive authority from the government to the politicians in a council which would (to their way of thinking) be controlled not by the chiefs but by elected members, who would be UNC leaders.

The powers transferred to district councils by the 1955 Ordinance made possible a further increase in the resources of the councils and so made them more attractive to any group anxious to wield power at district level. First, staff appointments became a council responsibility. The Lango Constitutional Regulations made under the 1955 Ordinance provided that the *rwot adwong* should be elected by the district council from among its senior officials. An appointments committee, elected by the council, assumed control over the appointment of all other staff (although subject to the Governor's final approval). In effect, therefore, as we have seen was the intention of the Ordinance, the chiefs became employees of the council, which assumed responsibility for appointments and dismissals. Understandably, the UNC councillors saw this as an important resource which they wished to control and the authority and powers of the appointments committee became a significant political issue.

Secondly, the Lango Regulations provided for an elected chairman of the council from among the council members, without restriction.

It thus became possible for an elected member to become chairman in place of a county chief. The UNC tried immediately after the 1956 elections to take over this office, when its unofficial members on the new council (elected through the indirect elections at sub-county level) nominated Engur as candidate for chairman. The latter obtained a majority of one vote in the first ballot (which may well have reflected support from Rwot Yakobo Adoko, who expected the UNC to support his claim to *won nyaci*). The officials in the council were still divided, however, and Yakobo's rival's votes tipped the scales; on the second and third ballots Engur was defeated by Nicholas Opio, the District Education Officer and also a member of the council.[45]

Engur's narrow defeat thus suggested that the UNC enjoyed the support of a number of officials who were not publicly associated with the party. Certainly the trend of the debate in the following two years suggested that some at least of the chiefs, as well as nominated members, were prepared increasingly to accommodate themselves to the party. Nevertheless the party at that stage had not gained control of the council. In spite of this, from 1956 onwards the UNC members increasingly dominated debate in the district council, which they used as a platform to demand further political change at national and local levels. They followed their 1955 resolution against the appoint-ment of an Asian minister with one in 1956 demanding direct elections for the whole country and another in 1958 calling on Buganda to cooperate with the other districts. At the same time, while demanding reforms in the central government, they initiated a campaign for the further politicization of the district council by proposing, at the May 1957 council meeting, that a *political* post of *won nyaci* should be established.[46]

Following a new proposal for a *won nyaci* the council appointed a constitutional committee which discussed not only that post, but also other institutional changes in the council including direct elec-tions and the separation of the posts of chairman and executive officer of the district administration. The debate within the committee, between the UNC and Jacobs, the District Commissioner, by all accounts became heated and acrimonious, generating a good deal of tension that overflowed into the council itself. It was complicated by the Protectorate government's decision in 1958 to abolish the appoint-ments committee and replace it by an appointments board, to which UNC councillors strongly objected as an infringement of the 'self-government' granted to the district council in 1955. Nevertheless, agreement was reached by the end of 1959 to introduce direct elections and an unofficial majority. The first direct elections were held in January 1960. The UNC swept the board, winning all but three of the

seats and thus assuming the majority position on the council. Milton
Obote, who had become the Lango representative in the Legislative
Council (to whom we shall return below), became chairman. From
this point the council was a UNC (and from March UPC)[47] body.
When at the May meeting Nicholas Opio, formerly chairman and
now a nominated member (and who in 1961 was to seek election to the
Legislative Council as a DP candidate), objected to the council's
proposals for the *won nyaci* and their nominations for the appointments board, Obote informed him from the chair that the council
elections 'were fought by two parties on different policies. The policy
of one party was accepted by the people and the sooner Mr Opio
accepted this as a fact the better'. The UNC had won its objective of a
directly elected district council controlled by themselves.

They had not, however, at that point achieved complete control,
for the proposal for a *won nyaci* was different from that for direct
elections. The amended regulations gazetted in September 1959,[48]
which presumably reflected some kind of agreement between the
Protectorate government and the Lango leaders, had altered the *rwot
adwong*'s title to that of *won nyaci*, and that of the district administration secretary to secretary-general. Both were to be appointed
by the appointments board (itself now under the direct authority of
the Governor). The *won nyaci* was thus the chief executive of the
district administration, but his position was that of a civil servant
rather than that of a politician. This was not what the UNC wanted.
Their objective remained an elected political executive and the
new council appointed a delegation, led by Obote, to take up the
issue with the Governor. This began further protracted negotiations
between the council and the Protectorate government, in which a
compromise was reached only in 1961. At that point the council
compromised over the *won nyaci* by accepting a ceremonial head of
district, elected by the council and thus a political post. The secretary-
general, as the chief executive officer, would be appointed by the
appointments board. A motion to establish the *won nyaci* as 'an
elected and constitutional and political head and number one man
in Lango and without executive powers' was passed at the May 1960
meeting of the council. After a good deal of argument about the
details of the appointment the Protectorate government agreed
although this meant retreating from their long-established policy
against district constitutional heads. The council anticipated agreement
(and at the same time pushed their case) by electing Engur (out of
prison for some time but no longer a member of the council) as
*won nyaci* in July 1960. At the beginning of 1961 the Protectorate
government finally agreed to his appointment and in February

Engur, as *won nyaci*, opened the council meeting. His election and assumption of office further symbolized the UPC's dominant hold on the district.[49]

The UPC had still failed, however, to obtain one important resource that they had demanded: the secretary-general, as the chief executive, remained a local government official, appointed by the appointments board and thus in theory outside politics. The campaign for the politicization of this post, therefore, continued. It was not won until after independence: three years later, in June 1963, the independent government amended the district administration legislation to provide for two new political posts, elected by the district council: a secretary-general who became responsible for the district administration as a whole, and a treasurer responsible for its finances.[50] Ben Otim became secretary-general and S. C. Okelo Olong (also associated with the party) treasurer. Thus the UPC's long battle for full political control came to an end only in 1963, when they had control of the offices of *won nyaci*, secretary-general, financial secretary, and chairman, all political posts and filled by party stalwarts.[51]

The early activity at district level, and the focus upon district political objectives, considerably influenced the style of UNC politics at district level and the structure of the party. First, in the 1950s in Lango the UNC was essentially a group of local leaders who dominated the local branch from its inception, although they had a very limited organization behind them. This was symbolized by the election of Engur as won nyaci in 1960. Second, although the party did not build up a large fee-paying membership, it did establish a good deal of rural sympathy and support, and therefore a mass base at the district level. Thus a not particularly sympathetic District Commissioner could say of the UNC in his 1957 District Report: 'In the same way that "bye-law" has become a Lango word meaning latrine so the word "Congress" had come to mean a political party . . .'. Although organizationally it was not a mass party, it had massive popular support in the rural areas. This was demonstrated by its successive electoral victories first in the indirect elections for the district council in 1956, and then the direct district elections of 1960; and secondly, in the 1958 direct elections for the Lango representative in the Legislative Council, when Milton Obote, the UNC candidate, won an overwhelming majority against three other candidates, each sponsored by a different party.[52]

With the UNC victory in the Legislative Council in 1958, the party also won control of the district's representation at the centre. This marked an important development for the branch and carried further implications for the leadership which have to be considered in relation to the role of the Legislative Councillor in Uganda as a whole at that date.

Until 1958 the UNC in Lango had enjoyed only limited access to the centre, primarily because the party headquarters in Kampala had not provided the communication or the organs through which access could be maintained. This had been true also of the other parties formed in this period. In the 1950s it was generally not party officials who provided effective communication between district and centre, but the African representative members whom Sir Andrew Cohen had introduced into the Legislative Council in 1953, elected by the district councils to represent the districts. Not all of these members had proved effective representatives but those who did very quickly assumed the dominant position as district spokesmen at the centre in the Legislative Council. It was this group which provided the national leadership for Africans at this time. Some of them belonged to the UNC but it was their membership of the Legislative Council, not their party affiliation, that gave them their standing and political position.

By 1956 the leading African representative members of the Legislative Council had established themselves as a cohesive opposition to the Protectorate government, working for the most part through their Unofficial Members' organization. They had challenged the constitutional changes proposed after the Namirembe Settlement of 1954. They had rejected the idea of a special position for Buganda, and the separate political development implied, especially the decision to hold direct elections in Buganda in 1957, four years before the rest of the country. The African members had accepted Sir Andrew Cohen's proposals for a unitary state; they therefore insisted on uniform treatment for all the districts and Buganda, in the first place with direct elections for the whole country. They won their point on direct elections for the whole country to which the government agreed, and which were held as a result in ten districts, including Lango, but excluding Buganda, in November 1958.[53] The Legislative Councillors therefore proved themselves important as district representatives and spokesmen for African interests; a district anxious to be heard at the centre needed in the first place, in the absence of a cohesive national party, an articulate member of the Council.

Mr Yakobo Omonya, Lango's representative on the Legislative Council since 1953, was neither a party (UNC) man nor articulate. He had never spoken in the Council. Lango UNC views on direct elections as well as other issues, therefore, were voiced at district level but not at the centre, so that not surprisingly by 1957 the UNC branch wanted to put a party man in his place. In May 1957 UNC members of the district council proposed that Milton Obote, recently returned from Kenya, should replace him. Some discussion followed and it was suggested that Omonya might be trained to become district judge. The district council then agreed without opposition to a proposal put forward by the UNC members that Mr Omonya should be asked to resign to become Lango's chief judge. In December 1957, at the last council meeting of the year, Milton Obote, a strong UNC member, was elected as his successor, and took his seat in the Legislative Council in March 1958.[54] This gave the UNC their link with the centre, in the Legislative Council, and thus control of district representation.

Obote, who like Engur was a nephew of Yakobo Adoko, had been one of the first Lango boys to reach Makerere, where he studied between 1947 and 1949.[55] In his 1958 election manifesto (when he stood for the Lango seat in Legislative Council) he claimed to have been engaged in Lango politics since 1949, when he had tried to obtain scholarships for Lango and had also taken up the issue of Lango boundaries. In 1952 he was writing to the *Uganda Herald* on political reform and criticizing the manner in which northern Uganda had been left behind.[56] He stood firmly in the centre of the younger, nationalist tradition. His activities between 1949 and 1956 are difficult to follow, and he himself has never been forthcoming. He left Makerere abruptly, before his examinations, in 1949, after which he worked for a construction company, first in Jinja and then in Kenya. But he maintained his connections with Uganda and certainly kept in close touch with Lango, and presumably therefore with Engur and the other UNC leaders when that party was established. While working in Kenya he became deeply engaged in Nairobi politics, joined the Kenya African Union (before it was proscribed in 1953), and later the Nairobi African Congress Party. When he returned to Lango late in 1956 his mind was clearly fixed on a political career in national Uganda politics. At first he remained behind the scenes advising Otim and the others on the line to adopt in the council. Within a short time however he began to accompany UNC delegations to the District Commissioner.[57] His actions suggested, however, that his objective was national, not district, political office. Since he was among the most educated Langi of that time and had had political experience in Kenya, it is not difficult to understand why the Lango UNC should see him as a more suitable representative than Mr Omonya on the Legislative Council. Engur, as the founder of the UNC in Lango, might perhaps have been preferred but he was at the time in jail, and in addition Obote's educational qualifications were superior.

But the UNC did not at that time have a clear majority on the district council and the earlier rivalry between the Yakobo Adoko family (to which Obote was related) and former Rwot Ogwangujji's family (to which Yakobo Omonya belonged) for dominance in the district had not ceased. Thus one might fairly ask how far Obote owed his original election to family support. It is possible that Yakobo Adoko (who had lost the post of *rwot adwong* in 1956 but was still a nominated member of the district council) still saw potential UNC support for his claims to the office of *won nyaci* if that post were established. Whether or not this was the case, it could only be to his family's advantage to have Obote, his kinsman, rather than Omonya as Lango's member of the Legislative Council, so that although no voting figures have survived it is by no means impossible that Obote's original election was the result of an alliance between the elected UNC members and the Adoko faction on the council.

Once elected, however, it is unlikely that Obote owed his subsequent dominance in the district to kin support. In the first place the broad nature of his and UNC support over the district makes it difficult to suggest that his popularity was due solely to membership of a particular family or clan. The district was not, moreover, unanimously in support of the former Rwot Yakobo Adoko. In the second place, once he had been elected to office, Obote very quickly emerged in his own right as a major nationalist politician. Lacking any strong 'charismatic' appeal, he won his dominant position by hard work and an intuitive awareness of how to appeal to local people.

Obote very quickly made his mark in the Legislative Council, emerging rapidly as one of the most prominent and politically radical of the African representative members. He joined George Magezi (Bunyoro), John Babiiha (Toro), Cuthbert Obwangor (Teso), John Lwamafa (Kigezi), and C. Katiti (Ankole) in their joint opposition to the Protectorate government's proposals which accorded Buganda separate political treatment from the rest of the country. In his first major speech in the Legislative Council he demanded that the implications of the Buganda Agreement for Uganda's development as a unitary state be recognized.[58] By 1959 he had emerged as the leader of the African unofficial members. At the same time he gained the dominant position in the major wing of the UNC in Kampala. He thus provided Lango with a highly effective spokesman at the centre.

Although he held no party office at district level, Obote, as the Lango member of the Legislative Council, took a full part in Lango UNC and district council affairs, acquiring a reputation as the one man who could control both party and council. As an *ex officio* member of the district council, he took a close interest in its activities, supporting the UNC group within it. As we have seen, he became chairman in 1960. When an issue arose between the Lango UNC and the administration, as, for example, over a suggestion that Nandi should be settled in the district in 1959, he led the UNC opposition.[59] In the Legislative Council he supported motions and resolutions concerned with the enlargement of the authority of the district councils. In 1958, for example, he strongly opposed the decision to replace the appointments committees with appointments boards, on the grounds that this took power away from the district council.[60]

He appeared very quickly to evolve a clear working relationship between himself as party and district spokesman at the national level, and the existing local branch leadership.[61] A clear division of responsibility was established between the two levels of leadership. There was no doubt about Obote's overall leadership in the district, which was demonstrated first by his election in 1958 and then by his assumption of the office of district council chairman in 1960. At the same time there was also no doubt about the function of the local leaders, who remained responsible for the continued work of the party at district level and within the district council.

This separation between a national and a district leadership became clearer in 1961, when the time came to select party candidates for the national elections to the enlarged Legislative Council. In Lango none of the local UNC leaders who had started the party in the district was selected for the four Lango seats. Instead three new men, all of them more educated than the existing district leadership, were chosen to stand with Obote for the Legislative Council. As a result the differentiation between district and national leadership and so the potential for party conflict was sharpened. The new elected members of the Legislative Council (who were re-elected to the National Assembly in the second election which followed a year later) had, however, to cooperate with the intermediary, district leadership to maintain their local party position and their rural base. This meant that they in turn required political resources at the district level. The politicization of the district council became an important asset in providing some of the necessary resources.

The party hold on the district depended on a complex system of relationships between the various levels of leadership which linked village with district and district with Kampala. From 1957 onwards Obote, as the member of the Legislative Council for Lango (and after 1961 leader of the Lango parliamentarians in Kampala), was the fulcrum around which the organization functioned. He controlled the district through the branch leadership; the branch leadership maintained communications with the lower levels through the councillors. Once the party assumed control of the district council it also had the hierarchy of chiefs as an additional structure through which control could be exerted, although the relationship between chiefs and party is a difficult one to disentangle.

The direct elections to the district council in March 1960 demonstrated that, although the party might not have an elaborate formal district machine, its leaders and followers were well organized. Thus, although the party was one of district notables rather than a mass party, it had established effective support through its informal contacts at grass roots level. This support, and the two tiers of leadership, were the major features of the Lango branch of the UNC at the time it was merged into the Uganda People's Congress when that party was formed in March 1960.

The Lango branch had developed to a very large extent as an autonomous unit; this autonomy was carried over into the new party. The activities of district party officials during the two years between the formation of the new party and independence, when national issues were being negotiated in Kampala and London, remained concentrated on the district. While the UPC leaders in Kampala bargained their way to independence, therefore, the UPC in Lango continued to fight on what were essentially district issues: the post of ceremonial head of the district, to which the government agreed in 1959 and to which Engur (not his uncle!) was elected in 1960; the campaigns to introduce elected unofficial members as chairmen of the lower level councils, to introduce free primary education, to abolish tax on cattle, and to obtain control of the appointments board; the demand for a political secretary-general, which the branch submitted to the Munster Commission. While all these issues had a national significance, they were local issues concerned also with the question of party power and patronage at the district level. Central party leaders had therefore to listen to their district leaders' demands if they wished to maintain the support of the district party leadership with whom their own position at district level was closely intertwined.

The growth of political party activity at the district level had also contributed greatly to the growth of nationalism in Lango. A word about the nature of this nationalism might be added. First, the idea of a national party, whose objective was self-government for Uganda, was introduced into Lango from Buganda. It was taken up enthusiastically by local Lango men but the original stimulus was from the south. Few of the local men who became associated with the UNC had contacts with other parts of the country but this did not prevent them from quickly accepting the idea of political change at the national level. They were thus willing and anxious to establish

nationalist politics in the district. They proceeded to seek these objectives between 1953 and 1956 with little further assistance from
UNC leaders in Kampala, who became engrossed in parochial (Ganda)
issues. Once Obote returned to Lango the district had a stronger link
with the party in Kampala, but at that stage the political action took
place in the Legislative Council rather than in the party organs.

These Lango leaders thus campaigned on the typical nationalist
demands of the terminal period of colonialism in terms of Uganda
independence. But they gave only a limited emphasis to the ideology
of colonial nationalism. There was very little ideological basis to
their campaign and, so far as it existed, the ideological basis was
linked with local rather than national issues. The Lango UNC aroused
a popular response to its ideas and demands for personal and civil
liberties because it translated these into local terms. In Lango this
meant an emphasis upon issues that affected a predominantly peasant
population; in this way the UNC created for itself the image of a
movement which had the well-being of the peasantry at heart. This
was the image which the UPC inherited.

None of this is surprising. It repeats a pattern that has now been
revealed as familiar in many parts of Africa, by which a nationalist
party aroused and maintained mass support by its espousal of parochial
issues which were more significant than national issues to the local
community.

Their electoral successes gave the UNC almost total control of
Lango District and both local and national representation. In January
1960 the UNC won all but three of the elected seats on the district
council. The Lango member of the Legislative Council was a UNC
member and the four Lango representatives elected to the enlarged
legislature in 1961 (and again in 1962) all belonged to the UPC. The
party won both national elections with large majorities for all four
seats. But they were not the only party in the district. In all these
elections, with the exception of Obote's constituency in 1961, there
were rival claimants. Other parties attempted to establish themselves
in the district and it is necessary to look briefly at them.

Three other parties set up branches in Lango between 1956 and
1957: the Progressive Party, the United Congress Party, and the
Democratic Party. The Progressive Party,[62] formed in 1955 by Eridadi
Mulira and other western-educated Ganda, and representing Ganda
Protestant schoolmasters, prosperous farmers, and African entre-
preneurs, stood for liberal political change but was generally more
conservative and less radical than the UNC. It looked generally to
schoolteachers for support; it failed to win any kind of following in
Lango as elsewhere. The party candidate Japhat Okae, a schoolmaster,

lost his deposit in the 1958 elections (against Obote), and shortly afterwards joined UNC. In 1961 he became one of the UPC's Lango MPs. The United Congress Party [63] was formed in Kampala in 1957 by a breakaway from the UNC by a group of its more educated leaders, partly for ideological reasons, partly out of criticism of UNC organization, and partly out of opposition to Musazi's leadership. Also appealing to the more educated, the schoolteachers, their candidate in Lango in 1958 also lost his deposit. The party aroused no local support.

The Democratic Party, however, survived and it is that party which provided such opposition as existed in the district, first to the UNC and then to the UPC. Its organizers and early supporters were, for the most part, schoolteachers from Catholic schools, particularly Ngetta Catholic mission just outside Lira. The party was from its inception generally viewed in Lango as a Catholic organization: an image later strengthened by the tendency of Kampala party officials, when they visited the district, to use the Roman Catholic mission as their base. Although the branch was established before the 1958 Legislative Council elections,[64] vocal DP supporters were early reported in only a small number of councils. In June 1957, for example, the Assistant District Commissioner reported that the DP was well represented in the Amach sub-county council, and that he had 'held the ring while they had a good go at the UNC members led by P. Okullo, over the senior secondary school'.[65] At this time DP supporters were also reported in Aboko council (in Moroto County) and at Minakula and Otual, both in Oyam County. All three were centres with a concentration of Catholics. Elsewhere there was little DP activity either in the council meetings or generally in the countryside. There were no reports of party meetings.[66] The party's heavy defeat in the 1958 election (when their candidate polled 7,000 against Obote's 40,000 votes) was the result not only of Obote's personal reputation but also of the DP's inability to match the informal but effective organization which the UNC had by that stage developed.[67] With improved organization and some assistance from Kampala party officials, the DP still failed, however, to win any parliamentary seats in the highly competitive years of 1961 and 1962, although they polled 20 per cent of votes in both elections.[68] Their only electoral success was three seats in the district council elections in 1960. In Lango District, therefore, unlike all other districts in Uganda, the DP failed to establish itself and the UPC had a monopoly of political power.

As we have noted earlier, the influence of religion on politics in Uganda has been almost unique in Africa.[69] The Democratic

Party emerged in the 1950s primarily in response to Roman Catholic fears of Protestant dominance, in Buganda and other districts, and with the support of Catholic missions. Some observers found a high correlation between religious affiliation and voting behaviour in the two national elections of 1961 and 1962.[70] Thus the fact that in Lango the Protestant population was generally double the Catholic, being 43 per cent against the latter's 21 per cent, would assist considerably in explaining the DP failure.[71] Only if the DP had been able to obtain the support of the 35 per cent listed as 'other' in the 1959 census could they have hoped to win any seats in Protestant-dominated constituencies. This they clearly failed to do. Significantly they won their three seats in the district council in that part of the district (Minakula) where Catholics formed a large proportion of the population.

Several other factors may also however have contributed to the UNC/UPC dominance and made it difficult for the DP to offer anything other than a religious appeal. First the UNC gained its initial ascendancy in the district before 1956, when the Catholics do not appear to have taken a great deal of interest in politics. When in 1952 a Catholic schoolteacher, Mr Acanga, complained that membership of the local councils was too much weighted in favour of Protestants, the District Commissioner, Powell-Cotton, suggested that the cause was lack of interest on the part of Catholics.[72] Acanga himself was originally a member of the Federation of Farmers and then of the UNC. Only in 1956, after he had spent some time in Kampala and met and talked to DP national leaders, did he leave UNC to organize a DP branch in Lira.[73] Second, there does not appear to have been in Lango District in these years the strong religious discrimination, or sense of discrimination, that would spark off conflict at any time. In 1956 there was strong local feeling against the Aler Farm School which was administered by the Verona Fathers Mission and the farm school itself was destroyed. The District Commissioner, however, thought this reflected feeling against the Verona Fathers as a foreign influence rather than against Catholics as such.[74] Complaints of religious discrimination were made after 1956 and the intense campaign conducted by the UPC in 1961 for the removal of Mr Omonya (a Catholic) from his post as chief judge, was interpreted as a party-religious issue. But generally there appeared to be fewer religious divisions in Lango than in many other districts.

Equally important is the fact that there were in Lango society as a whole few other obvious cleavages that might have formed a basis for party competition. Although there was a good deal of talk of clan rivalries in the late 1940s, there is little evidence to support the view that they produced serious internal cleavages in the district. But however much clan support might have been significant in local politics, clan rivalries did not in the 1950s provide a basis for inter-party rivalries: leading members of many clans joined the UNC, and later the UPC. The contest between Rwot Yakobo Adoko and his supporters and Rwot Ogwangujji and his suggests that what administrative officers regarded as clan may well have been a question of kin. There were also few glaring economic divisions within the community. Few Langi in the 1950s stood out from their neighbours by virtue of their assets. There was an air of economic equality in the district as a whole, in a basically peasant community in which each man cultivated a small plot. The chiefs were generally a privileged community, economically better off than other members of the tribe, able to live better and to educate their families in a manner that the majority of the community could not afford, and the popular antagonism towards the chiefs which the UNC exploited in the early 1950s was in some respects an antagonism towards a growing privileged class. Otherwise there were no deep economic divisions which the DP could exploit. UNC and DP party policies, generally, differed very little in this period.

Other factors besides the absence of serious internal cleavages within the society help to explain the undivided control which the UNC acquired over Lango but not over other districts. First, the local branch leadership undoubtedly built up a considerable local sympathy and support between 1953 and 1958 which later stood the UNC and then the UPC in good stead. While they lacked a strongly organized party machine they had the council system through which to maintain their position. Second, from 1958 onwards, Obote's position in Uganda politics was a major asset for the UNC in Lango itself. Once he had assumed a position of prominence at the centre it was unlikely that the Langi would withdraw their support from him, and therefore from the party he supported, for he offered them a real opportunity to obtain a position of influence, if not control, in central government institutions. This undoubtedly contributed a great deal to the continued dominance of the UPC after 1960.

Nationalist politics in Lango were therefore, before independence, scarcely competitive party politics. In this respect Lango was atypical, since elsewhere in Uganda a strong two-party system emerged. Acholi District, the second northern district which is considered here, amply demonstrates the growth of inter-party politics at district level in the second half of the 1950s.

# 5

# POLITICS IN ACHOLI DISTRICT 1945–1962

With the exception of Lango, and indeed Buganda, between 1958 and 1962 the district became in Uganda a political arena for strong competitive party politics between the UNC (and later the UPC) and the DP, as a result of which Uganda became a vigorous competitive two-party state. This political competition emerged as the main characteristic of the party system that developed in Acholi, to which district we now turn. When the Acholi branch of the UNC was formed in 1953 its early activities followed a pattern similar to that established in Lango. The new party recruits there directed their activities against the administration and the Acholi local government because, as in Lango, that body provided a forum at a time when there was no national forum in which they could make themselves heard. Unlike the Lango leaders, however, the Acholi UNC did not have a monopoly of political activity since the DP, formed three years after the UNC, also acquired a following in the district and the district council. In looking at post-war politics in Acholi we shall therefore concentrate on those features that contribute to our understanding of this growth of inter-party politics at district level.

Acholi, the second largest district in Uganda, is a vast area with a scattered population. Gulu, the headquarters of the Northern Province as well as of the district, was not in the late 1940s very much larger than Lira. It had a smaller trading but a larger official community, as befitted its position as the provincial headquarters. The great majority of the Acholi, like the rest of the population of the north, were small farmers, growing cotton and (in the west) some tobacco as well as food crops. In the early 1940s they had suffered heavier losses of cattle from disease and drought than the Langi, as a result of which their cattle trade diminished greatly. The general economic background against which Acholi politics developed after the War was nevertheless very similar to that of Lango; a slowly expanding peasant economy with an agricultural and commercial potential largely unrealized because of the limitations of labour, capital, and internal communications.

The Acholi political background was however significantly different; Acholi was politically much more complex and less homogeneous than Lango.[1] First the district was internally divided into a

number of chiefdoms, which the British in the 1950s erroneously
called clans. The concept of 'Acholi' had not in fact existed before the
first Europeans entered the area, when they mistook the Acholi for the
Shilluk, with the result that 'Shuli' became 'Acholi'. At the time of
the British occupation Acholi had evolved a more centralized political
organization than Lango, of which the basic unit was the chiefdom.
There were nine large chiefdoms, Atyak, Pabo, Padibe, Paranga,
Pajule, Lira Palwo, Koic, Payera, and Patiko; clustered around each of
these larger states were numerous small chiefdoms technically independent but with something of a client relationship towards them.
Historically there was considerable rivalry between these chiefdoms,
the most important being between Payera, which by 1880 had expanded to become the largest, and the rest. These rivalries continued into
the colonial period. In addition the Acholi were also divided by complex descent patterns, the nine large chiefdoms having different
origins, on the basis of which they were divided into three groups,
one predominantly Madi in blood, and only lately 'Lwoized', the
second group with strong Karamajong (Paranilotic) origins, and the
third a mixed group with quite separate origins. Two of the chiefdoms,
Pajule and Lira Palwo, had strong Bunyoro connections. These
different origins and royal connections went far to determine alliances
between the different chiefdoms. Superimposed upon these traditional
political divisions was a strong religious cleavage between Catholic
and Protestant, the result of intense missionary activity, particularly
on the part of the Catholic Verona Fathers.

Initially the British had sought to use the traditional chiefs or
*rwodi* of the major chiefdoms whom they elevated over the smaller
groups. The counties, which bore the names of the major chiefdoms,
each included a number of the smaller client states. This in turn created
additional sources of tension. By 1937 however the attempt to ad-
minister through traditional chiefs had been abandoned. The counties
which included a number of chiefdoms were renamed after geographical features instead of the old chiefdoms. Most of the men
subsequently appointed as county chiefs were in fact members of one
or another of the traditional ruling or 'royal' families but they were
not necessarily appointed to their own areas, being instead moved
around a great deal. Thus a county chief did not necessarily have any
traditional legitimacy in the area for which he was administratively
responsible. Since traditional chieftaincy loyalties remained strong this
created greater and continuing chiefdom rivalries, which contributed
further to district cleavages and internal political rivalries. In the
general competition for position and office, rivalry both within and
between chiefdoms was of much greater political significance than

was the case in Lango. In 1958 for example the District Report referred to the tendency in the district council to split into groups on clan (meaning chiefdom), religious party, or territorial patterns. 'Members have tended to consider themselves representatives not only of the area from which they come but also of the particular group to which they are aligned by clan or religion.'

The council system established in Acholi in the mid-1940s differed from that in Lango in two main respects. First, councils were not created at the parish level until 1950 and, second, both in the parish and higher councils the elected members were until 1955 (when the system was reorganized under the 1955 Ordinance) chiefdom heads elected from among their own numbers by all the chiefdom heads of the area. Thus although the experiment of the 1930s which had attempted to base administration on traditional leaders had been abandoned as a failure, there was still a predilection to incorporate as many traditional elements as possible into the governmental structure. Only in 1955 were un-officials elected freely from all taxpayers and special chiefdom represen-tatives abandoned. The district council established under the 1949 African Local Government Ordinance consisted of sixteen *ex officio* members (the county chiefs, the local government officers, and the senior *jagi*), eight members nominated by the district council and eight by the District Commissioner, and twenty-two elected by the chiefdom heads.[2] The membership included some of the younger, educated men in the community, such as J. Abe, a young schoolteacher, and O. L. Lalobo, an agricultural officer, both associated with the Young Acholi Association; the Provincial Commissioner believed the composition of the council therefore satisfied the 'radicals' of that body who had objected to rule through the clan heads. Notwithstanding this official view council membership was still weighted on the side of officialdom and local traditional chiefdom leadership.[3] In the 1940s it was a lively body, somewhat preoccupied with staff appointments (on which the members voted) and staff allowances and salaries.[4] By 1950 however there was more debate over a wider variety of district affairs: the agenda for the April 1950 meeting for example included agricultural, leprosy, and health bye-laws; scholarships for non-Acholi resident in the district; a national park at Anaka; the Crown forest reserve at Kilak Hills; and methods of selecting chiefs.

The most politically vocal group in the immediate post-war years were the county chiefs, who, like their counterparts in Lango, were anxious to obtain greater powers for the Acholi African Local Government and thereby greater authority for themselves. The se-quence of events was similar to that in Lango, although the campaign was complicated by the long-established contest between Padibe,

Payera, and Pajule for a paramountcy over Acholi as a whole. In 1944 the chiefs on the council began to campaign for the appointment of a secretary-general, similar to the post created in Teso.[5] In this they had the support of those unofficial members of the district council representing the more educated element in the community. The debate continued despite the refusal of the provincial administration and the government to consider the request, and at the October 1948 annual council meeting a motion was passed proposing that Acholi should have a secretary-general or president and an Acholi (district) judge. The 1949 Annual Report referred to continued thinking about the question of a paramount chief.[6] A visit by a group of councillors for Teso, Mbale, Busoga, Buganda and Bunyoro in 1950 stimulated a fresh demand for a constitution similar to that of Teso.[7]

Over this period the Acholi chiefs encountered the same official opposition to the idea of a paramount chief as had their counterparts in Lango. Speaking to the district council meeting of April 1949 the District Commissioner announced:

It will not be permitted to try and make a sort of hereditary king whose family would become rulers. This would not be at all in accordance with modern ideas and the intention of giving the people more say in their own government.[8]

Specifically the administration rejected claims of either Payera or Padibe chiefdoms to a paramountcy over the whole district. At the same time however, the chiefs found the provincial administration anxious to establish more effective communication between local and central government, and to effect the reorganization necessary to meet the changes of the 1949 Ordinance. As a result in 1950 a compromise was effected, which established two new posts very similar to those in Lango: the *lawirwodi* who would be both chairman of the district council and also senior executive officer of the Acholi local government and the *langolkop madit*, chief judge, in charge of the district's courts. Both posts would be elected by the district councillors from among the county chiefs.[9] Rwot Lamot of Adilang became the first *lawirwodi* and Rwot Yona Odida of Payera *langolkop*.

The post of *lawirwodi* did not carry with it the extensive powers some of its exponents had associated with the concept of a paramount, but it did carry much greater powers than had hitherto been enjoyed by any local government official. The *lawirwodi* also in a short time grew in status, particularly as the provincial administration viewed him as the main link between Protectorate and Acholi local government. Competition for the position consequently became a significant element in Acholi politics, arousing considerable chiefdom rivalry, the more intense because three of the county chiefs at this time were also men with a claim to hereditary chiefdomship. A good deal of local interest, similar to that in Lango, focused upon office in the Acholi local government, thus emerged. Thus Matayo Lamot of Agago, and traditional rwot of Adilang, a 'client state', lost the post in 1953 to Philip Adonga MBE, county chief of Chua, and of the Pajule royal family, who was voted in as *lawirwodi*. Matayo Lamot returned to his post of county chief of Agago.

At the same time popular interest developed in the lower level councils. Again the situation was comparable to Lango. In 1951 the District Commissioner reported that it was 'difficult to get Council Members to understand that their powers are limited and to make them see they have no right to overrule Government policy or the decision of higher Councils'.[10] Thus by the early 1950s considerable attention was focused on local government institutions; although the debate was dominated by chiefdom heads.

Party politics began in Acholi in 1953, when, after a visit by Musazi and Mayanja, a branch of the UNC was formed at a large meeting held in Gulu. A young man called Peter Oola became chairman, and other officials included E. Lajul, then working in the Uganda Book-shop, G. Latim, a trader, and Okot B'tek, then a schoolteacher. In the early years however the Gulu committee proved of signal unimportance in establishing party activity. It was Oola rather than the committee who established the UNC in Acholi. Soon after he had started the party branch however he was arrested for his alleged part in fomenting a strike of local workers in Gulu early in 1953, so his activities came to a halt. Released from jail within a few months, after acquittal on appeal to the High Court, he returned not to Gulu but to Kitgum in East Acholi, and this latter centre remained his base for the following two years. The UNC as a result emerged as a local movement in Kitgum and East Acholi earlier than in the western part of the district. Political party activity developed in West Acholi only from 1955.

Oola's background made him a likely person to gravitate to the new-style politics, not least because he had had considerable contacts with the world outside Acholi. After leaving Gulu High School in 1943, he served in the King's African Rifles until the end of the War. He then spent several years working in Kenya, where he was associated with Kenya's African politicians and learned his politics in the Euro-pean-dominated Nairobi of those years. Returning to Acholi in 1951 he joined the Public Works Department but a year later when he met Musazi and came into touch with the newly formed UNC in Kampala, he left his job to start the party branch in Gulu.

A second prominent figure in East Acholi in the early formative years, Otema-Alimadi, had a similar background. He was an Army Medical Corps dresser, before returning to work in the medical service in Uganda and then in Acholi as a dresser. At the time the UNC branch was established he was working in a dispensary in Palabek, where he was covertly very much involved in the new party's activities. Later he returned to West Acholi where he emerged as a prominent party figure and rival to Oola.

At Kitgum in 1954 Oola set up a local committee, consisting of a leader from each sub-division, each of whom was then left to establish subordinate groups in the smaller centres and villages. These local leaders were predominantly small traders and farmers. The chairman of UNC in Padibe, Samson Ocan, was a farmer; in Madei, Opei Belesio Okwok had been both a catechist teacher and a village chief before retiring to farming. In Palabek the first chairman, Yonasai Aruch, had been a station sergeant in the police, and had worked in Kegezi, Toro, and Buganda. A good number of other original UNC supporters had also had police experience and a good number had been in the KAR. At a later date the party was to receive considerable support from teachers whom the provincial administration regarded as 'very political' but during the first three years this group did not come forward openly, perhaps for fear of dismissal.

Oola and his fellow workers at county and lower levels encountered more difficulties than their counterparts in Lango. In the early days of the UNC in Lango there had been some degree of cooperation between the new party leaders and the administration. The District Commissioner had received them in his office and there had been no restrictions upon public meetings. It was only after the disturbance at Lira at the end of 1956 that the provincial administration became openly hostile towards local party spokesmen. In Acholi, on the other hand, the administration was from the outset antagonistic towards and distrustful of the new party.[11] The chiefs, who appeared to have a tighter control of the councils than in Lango, were more hostile and were encouraged by the provincial administration to oppose the party.[12] In 1954, for example, the district council passed a resolution against public meetings outside Gulu and Kitgum,[13] a restriction lifted only in 1956. When Oola applied for permission to hold a meeting in the Kitgum area in November 1954 he was told by the Assistant District Commissioner that he himself was holding a public *baraza* at Labongo at that time, which Oola could attend and at which he could raise any questions which he wished. 'As the Acholi Councils have stated that they do not want you to hold meetings,' he concluded, 'I do not feel justified in going against their wishes by allowing you to hold a meeting, but at the baraza you will have the opportunity of clarifying points on which you are not clear.'[14] Whether or not Oola attended the meeting is unknown. What is clear is that in the early years it was extremely difficult to hold public rallies outside Kitgum or Gulu. Not surprisingly, therefore, he and the other party activists concentrated on small informal meetings in people's houses in the villages, an approach very similar to that adopted in Lango.

The local leadership set out to build grass roots support in this way by challenging colonial policy and articulating local grievances. They were more secretive than the leaders in Lango, to avoid too much open conflict with the provincial administration and the chiefs. Perhaps not surprisingly, therefore, these early activities are today recalled as essentially conspiratorial, at least until 1958 when the district council lifted its ban on meetings in the rural areas. In spite of official opposition, however (or perhaps because of it) the Kitgum group successfully established support at the village level, and aroused strong sympathy for the movement, if they did not collect a large number of party subscriptions. Peter Oola's arrest and imprisonment in 1953 aroused curiosity and stimulated additional support. Thus by November 1954, a year after the party had begun, administrative officers were describing questions at the lower level council meetings as 'Congress inspired', and reported that 'some were put up by known supporters of Congress'.[15] The successful build-up of support was demonstrated by the fact that, even without party organization or a formal party machine, several UNC supporters were elected to the district council in the 1955 elections, including some of the original East Acholi Committee.[16] These councillors frequently became important local leaders and political communicators, working through similar networks to those used by councillors in Lango.

Similar grass roots activity and support developed in West Acholi after 1955, when the branch leaders then expanded party influence rapidly. By 1959 the provincial administration reported that the UNC were strong in the district and represented in 'councils at all levels'.[17] A new kind of political leadership at the local level consequently emerged in response to party developments. The farmer or trader who became the local political leader was one of the most influential men in the county. In 1961 the District Commissioner summed up the situation when he wrote 'Usually there are three to six people in each division who seem to do all the leading and talking. There is no local opinion except what is formed and led by these local leaders. The local leaders tend to be the local party leaders.'[18] He was in particular speaking about Agago, but the Assistant District Commissioner reported the same kind of situation in Lamwo County, where the outstanding personalities tended 'to be the local party leaders', the UNC (by then the UPC) men. Usually there were three to six people who 'did all the leading'.[19]

Out of this activity a district leadership, with Oola at its head, provided the UNC with the same pattern of organization and support as emerged in Lango. The support was primarily from the farmers and traders of the rural areas. In the background, not openly associated with the branch, but assisting them and supporting their stand in the councils, were some of the emerging group of educated Acholi, some of whom were nominated members of the district council. The party also had the covert support of certain Acholi departmental officers.[20] Thus the district party leadership was probably more broadly based than it was in Lango.

During this formative period the Acholi UNC lacked extensive links with the centre, and their activities were scarcely controlled by the party headquarters in Kampala. Peter Oola made regular visits to Kampala to attend executive meetings. He was a member of the UNC delegation to London in 1955. His visits were more important because they enabled him to keep in touch with events at the centre rather than enabling the centre to control the district. The Acholi member of the Legislative Council was not a member of the UNC but the district treasurer, Antony Opwa, formerly a county chief. Later in 1958, when Oola won the first directly elected seat on the Legislative Council, he became a more prominent link between district and centre—but through the Legislative Council rather than the central organs of the party. Thus the Acholi branch of the UNC grew very much as an autonomous unit, linked with the centre through the person of Oola, whose association with other Legislative Councillors in Kampala provided the main channel for local-central communication. The district leadership was only marginally controlled from Kampala.

When in 1961 the time came for the party to put forward parliamentary candidates for election, the district leadership was partly replaced (as was the case in Lango) by a new group of younger more educated men, recently returned from abroad. In East Acholi the key figure was Eric Lakidi, from Palabek, who had been educated and had taught in the Southern Sudan in the mid-1950s. On his return in 1956 he taught and then became assistant treasurer in the Acholi local government. In 1958-59 he studied public administration in Britain, after which he worked in the administration until 1961 when he resigned to stand for election. Although he had not previously been publicly involved in politics he had occupied a prominent role in his community and once he entered politics he quickly assumed the leadership of East Acholi UPC. Elected for North Acholi constituency he became a key political link between Kampala and Gulu.[21] In West Acholi the most important newcomer was Alex Ojera, a Payera man like Peter Oola, recently returned from studies abroad, who successfully contested the South-West Acholi seat in 1961, and so also became an important link between district and centre. Peter Oola's defeat by the DP in the other West Acholi constituency left him at the district level. Thus a similar division between district and national leadership emerged as in Lango, resulting however in more open and obvious friction between the two groups. The district leaders in Acholi were less ready to accept the subordinate position than the same group in Lango, perhaps in part because (as will be seen below) the existence of traditional chiefdoms whose support had to be wooed and won meant that the district leaders could not expect to monopolize the resources available at district level.

The UNC platform in Acholi as it emerged in the 1950s was characteristically the same combination of national and local issues that emerged in Lango. Oola and his colleagues were in the first place determined to add their voice to the demand for self-government. His first memorandum to the provincial administration, for example, concluded:

We consider the system of this country is not in the manner [sic] and that the Uganda Government should assist in a solution. We believe the transmission of political rights to the Uganda Government will help speed our advancement to self-government which is our greatest need and legitimate right.[22]

When he gave evidence to the Dreschfield Committee in 1954, at an open meeting in Gulu, he put forward the idea of a 'Central Native Assembly' for the Protectorate, of elected representatives from the whole country, to bring people into closer touch with each other. At their public meetings in Kitgum and Gulu he and other UNC leaders demanded their 'political rights', including direct elections[23] and challenged the appointment of the Asian, Mr (later Sir) Amar Maini, as minister in 1955.[24] Similar views were aired at meetings of lower level councils. Thus at the time that general opposition developed to the government's proposal to hold direct elections in Buganda before the rest of the country, at the county council meeting in Obyen

Three or four U.N.C. members protested strongly against the Governor's speech on direct election, and accused him of deliberately splitting the country and holding back the people of the country. The majority were very interested and supported the Congress view.[25]

Interest in the Legislative Council was evident in the local UNC reaction to Sir Andrew Cohen's proposed constitutional reforms of 1955, which the UNC leaders took as meaning they would be able to elect a new Acholi member to the Council. Oola called a meeting in August 1955 'of all Acholi in Gulu and Kitgum who pay taxes' to elect a representative from a number of candidates proposed by UNC. The District Commissioner rapidly disabused them of their idea, pointing out that Mr Opwa continued as member for the life of the Council.[26]

At the same time UNC leaders also demanded the democratization of the district council and the removal of the influence of the chiefs. A petition to the Governor in June 1956, therefore, not only included a request for direct elections throughout Uganda in 1957 but also for the reform of the Acholi local government.[27] One of their first meetings, held in Gulu in April 1953, had resolved that the Acholi people were not properly represented in the standing committee of the African local government and had opposed the method of nominating African members (who were civil servants) to the township authority. Thus 'The Protectorate Government through its officials . . . had combined with a group of teachers, chiefs and some of the Indian traders in both the Councils and the Township Authority . . .' What they objected to was official and chiefly dominance in the Acholi local government.[28]

The UNC also took up a variety of local grievances both at district rallies and in the lower level councils. Thus their spokesmen criticized cotton prices and marketing facilities; objected to the absence of medical facilities and demanded additional dispensaries; challenged the system by which education bursaries were awarded; objected to the restrictions upon freedom of movement imposed by local chiefs; opposed the forced labour required in Acholi as in Lango; the habit of administrative officers on tour of asking for food at reduced rates; the proposals for an Acholi national park; the Lipan game reserve in East Acholi; and the land tenure proposals of 1955. The combination of nationalist and parochial grievances was summed up in the list of subjects discussed at a UNC meeting in Kitgum in August 1957: direct elections; the number of representatives for Acholi; direct elections to the district council; free trade; eviction of Indians from trading centres; Padibe dispensary.[29] The position adopted by the Acholi branch might also, therefore, be considered typical of an African nationalist movement asserting itself against the colonial authorities and seeking to establish its legitimacy in the eyes of the public. Leaders appealed to local interests to stimulate support for nationalist demands. Later they discussed questions of constitutional reform raised in the Wild Report, including that of local and central government powers. In this way they articulated national issues in the locality. Since the provincial administration also used the district and lower level councils to publicize the constitutional and political issues then under debate, there was ample opportunity for people at the village level to become acquainted with the national political issues that were being debated in the Legislative Council in Kampala.

The evidence of official touring reports from 1953 onwards (which were written by administrative officers who did not necessarily have any sympathy for the new political leadership asserted by the UNC) suggests that there was a genuine popular response to the issues raised by the UNC and that this grew steadily throughout the 1950s. As a consequence by 1958 there was widespread interest in the first direct elections. 'I was impressed by the interest of ordinary people in the elections' one assistant district commissioner reported in February 1958.[30] Thus the foundations of the mass support for the party demonstrated by the 1961 and 1962 elections were laid.[31]

Certain issues aroused more popular support than others, and more positive response to the bid for political leadership that the branch was making. The first was land, and in particular the land tenure proposals of 1955, to which the Acholi, like the Langi, objected strongly. In the mid-fifties there was no shortage of land in the district, nor real cause for any lack of security. Land was still held under customary tenure, which provided complete security for the individual cultivating a plot. The lower councils had to be consulted over any proposal for alienation for public purposes, such as the creation of a forest reserve. There ought therefore to have been every sense of security. The reality was very different. Any government proposal that involved land aroused intense popular suspicion and opposition. At the public meeting in Gulu with the Dreschfield Committee, in July 1954, this suspicion was vigorously articulated in opposition to proposed local government land controls. Strong objections were voiced to the proposals in the Bill for the central control of crown land, because

the Acholi people want to have absolute right over their land. We will accept advice only from Her Majesty's Government on important decisions concerning land. Any power over land should only be delegated to the Governor or Provincial Commissioner or the District Commissioner by the Acholi. Any power over land now being invested in the Governor or the Provincial Commissioner is regarded with suspicion.[32]

Administrative officers on tour found themselves regularly asked questions about land, and the extent of the concern is suggested by the fact that objections to and fears of the land provisions in the 1955 District Councils Ordinance were expressed at divisional and lower level councils as well as in Gulu. Thus the Assistant District Commissioner, Fulford-Williams, reported on his tour of Obyen Division in June 1955 that he was asked 'whether it was true that the District Councils Ordinance would hand over the Acholi land to foreigners'.[33]

Suspicions about land were deep-rooted and they made people at grass roots level quick to react to any action at either district or national level on the matter. Such suspicions were particularly intense in East Acholi because of the local belief that the highlands in the northern part of the district were an object of European desire. The UNC articulated these suspicions and challenged any government action that appeared to threaten Acholi possession of their land. At an early Kitgum rally in January 1955 for example they passed a resolution against 'Europeans walking around our land', an objection to geological survey parties in the area.[34] They also opposed the idea of a game reserve at Lipan. Most important, in 1956, both inside and outside the district council, they vigorously opposed the Protectorate government's land tenure proposals.[35] As in Lango, it was this championship, according to many of their supporters, that won them much of their popular grass roots support. The UNC leaders claimed the government's withdrawal of the proposals as their victory, and in one supporter's view 'from there the people knew that the U.N.C. was the right thing'. At the time of the 1958 Legislative Council elections, they also exploited the association of their DP opponent, Antony Opwa, with the government to brand him with responsibility for these land proposals and so with a willingness to turn Acholi into another Kenya.[36]

A second specific grievance which the UNC successfully articulated arose out of the position and functions of the chiefs, and the manner in which the chiefs' authority impinged on the daily life of the people. There was much about the native administration system and the chiefs' authority that the ordinary people disliked. They did not for example like the system of unpaid labour; they had the same objections as Lango people to the way chiefs collected taxes and imposed agricultural rules. In 1955 there were objections to the manner in which many chiefs manipulated the system of indirect elections to see their own candidates returned to the different councils.[37] Thus there was a strong rural discontent with the rule of the chiefs and Oola and local UNC leaders won support because they articulated that discontent. The UNC challenged the chiefs on the grounds of incompetence, inefficiency, inability to change with the times, and oppressive behaviour towards the rural population. They challenged their dominant position in the councils, and demanded that council members should be elected directly by the people. These criticisms of the native administration won the UNC sympathy and support as the champions of the people against officialdom.

The UNC leaders were bound to challenge the chiefs for local leadership, as were the UNC in Lango. In some parts of the district they appear to have replaced them as the legitimate local leaders in the popular mind with remarkable ease. If the administrative officer was to be believed, in Palabek, for example, by 1956, the UNC 'had more control and influence and certainly more ability than the local chiefs'.[38]

Another issue that won the UNC considerable popular support in East Acholi but at the same time provoked internal division within the party itself was the status of that part of the district. There had always been a strong cleavage between the East and West, based upon both chiefdom rivalries and a sense in the eastern area that they were neglected. Until 1938 Acholi had been administered as two separate districts, Gulu and Chua, the latter with its headquarters at Kitgum. Their amalgamation into one district in 1938 had not established a greater sense of unity between the two areas. The people of East Acholi felt a strong resentment at the loss of their district status, which was increased by their sense of neglect in favour of the West. There were fewer local government services in the East, and poor communications made its geographical isolation appear all the greater. The more extensive educational development in West Acholi, arising out of earlier and more extensive mission activity around Gulu, had given that area greater opportunities, and men from Koich, Patiko, and Payera chiefdoms tended to predominate in jobs requiring educational qualifications. Thus Easterners also felt discriminated against in this respect.[39] This feeling of neglect was not dispelled by the upgrading of Kitgum to sub-district status in 1952. Instead there remained a strong sentiment among the 'Easterners' that they were receiving second-class treatment; a sentiment fostered to some extent by the desire of leaders of Padibe, the most influential chiefdom in East Acholi, to enjoy a greater status in the district as a whole.

It was natural that the UNC in East Acholi should support demands for improved services in the area. Thus for example on one occasion Oola and leaders from Labongo, Padibe, and Palabek journeyed all the way to meet the District Commissioner and the District Medical Officer in Gulu to demand that a proposed new government dispensary should be relocated at Padibe. There were numerous other petitions of this kind.[40] But the UNC was also drawn into the campaign for a separate district that was revived in 1957 and which aroused a great deal of popular local interest.[41] In 1958 both the general purposes committee of the Acholi District Council, and the council itself, debated and passed a proposal for a separate district created out of the three eastern counties. The central government refused however to agree to a resolution that a district headquarters should be established at Kitgum.[42] At the end of the year an East Acholi Association was formed to press for this object. Belesio Okwok, one of the local UNC leaders, was chairman, and several other UNC members were among its founders. Called a 'non-political movement' and including Democratic Party supporters, it was essentially a local movement, articulating East Acholi's sense of discrimination, and its members in the Kitgum area actively took up local complaints with the government.[43] In 1961 the Association presented a memorandum to the Relationships Commission stating their grievances and requesting a separate district, a request the Commission did not endorse.[44]

The demand for a separate district presented a serious problem for Acholi's UNC leadership, and subsequently for the national leadership of the UPC. The UNC did not wish to lose East Acholi support but to acquiesce to the East Acholi claim was to endanger its support in the western part of the district. The formation of the East Acholi Association therefore produced internal pressures that threatened branch unity. At a time when a second party, the Democratic Party, was seeking followers in East Acholi, UNC leaders from that area could not, however, ignore these claims and the East Acholi Association supporters included the leading UNC men of the area, such as Eric Lakidi, who later emerged as the dominant UNC figure in the East.[45] Both UPC and DP supporters signed the 1961 memorandum requesting a separate district, in spite of the fact that this represented a challenge to UPC party policy which was opposed to the creation of new districts.[46] It is a measure of the UNC's strength in the district as a whole that the branch did not split irrevocably on east-west lines. But the potential division was none the less there. The resultant frictions weakened the party and affected its position in the district council as well as in the national elections of 1961 and 1962.[47]

Once UNC supporters gained access to the district council in 1956 they used that body as a forum from which to articulate these various issues and to fight for greater power. In particular they took up three issues all connected with the campaign for control of the district government: changes in the structure and constitution of the district administration, and especially direct elections for the district council; staff appointments; and the post of *laloyo* or district head.

On the question of direct elections there was in fact no real conflict. The provincial administration was itself in favour of this change, and by 1958 the chiefs on the council had been forced to admit defeat. A more serious conflict concerned the method of appointment of staff, especially the chiefs. This issue had first emerged at the time of the Dreschfield inquiry, when that committee appeared in Gulu to hear views about the proposed local government legislation. The appointment of chiefs was officially regarded as fundamental to the legislation. The chiefs were to be primarily the servants of the district administration, so that they ought to be appointed by the district council. The question was who in the council. The councils understandably wanted the power for themselves, not a committee appointed by the central government. The UNC in particular wanted appointments controlled by the *elected* element in the council, a demand they publicized at their meetings.[48] After a good deal of debate, not only in Acholi but in all districts, the view prevailed that an appointments committee set up by the district council would have virtually complete authority over appointments.[49] As a result the new Acholi district council of 1956, on which the UNC had considerable influence, had the last word in the selection of the appointments committee and thus on the appointment of local government staff.

The district council of 1956 was hardly a party council. Elections had been indirect and there was still a dominant official influence,[50] so that the UNC could scarcely be said to control the council. But there were known UNC members and also a number of UNC sympathizers, some of whom became members of the appointments committee. Most of these were Protestants, and most were associated with the Bobi-Koich chiefdom of West Acholi. This group quickly began to assert themselves in relation to appointments. The council thus became a battleground between UNC supporters and the official element for the dominant influence over the appointment of staff. At the first meeting of the council the new UNC councillors challenged the officials (both of the district and the provincial administration) on two issues. First, they disagreed with the new council regulations drawn up by the standing committee, on which they alleged that the District Commissioner had rejected their views out of hand. These allegations were dismissed as unjustified but the issue remained a source of dissension between elected and official members. Second, they questioned certain staff appointments. They objected specifically to the continuation in the office of district treasurer of Antony Opwa, a Catholic from East Acholi, who was the Acholi member of the Legislative Council and a member of the government.[51] They alleged that Opwa had failed to do the job and petitioned the District

Commissioner to this effect in February 1956, arguing that Opwa could not effectively be both district treasurer and a member of the Legislative Council. Although they could not themselves dismiss Opwa, they sustained an intense campaign to secure his removal which reached a climax when the UNC councillors moved a resolution in the district council against his continued employment on the grounds of his inefficiency and that he used his office to his own private advantage. They also argued that the Treasurer should be elected in the same way as the *lawirwodi* and *angol-kop*.

The conflict over staff appointments quickly became a three-cornered one, since it involved not only the UNC and officials but also spokesmen of the newly-formed DP which in 1956 took up the cudgels against the UNC on the grounds of religious discrimination. These charges arose out of the fact that Opwa's critics were not only UNC, but also Protestant, and predominantly from one area, the Bobi-Koich chiefdom.

It was not surprising that such charges should be made in a district deeply divided on religious grounds. Catholics were a considerable majority (30 per cent) over Protestant (22 per cent). Each had a large mission at Gulu and numerous centres throughout the district although the Verona Fathers were much more numerous than the Protestants. They had a second major concentration around their mission at Kalongo in East Acholi, whose members were very politically conscious, several openly engaging in what could be termed political activities. Missionary activity, both Protestant and Catholic, had begun earlier in West than in East Acholi, so that there was a larger concentration of educational activity in the West, and men from West Acholi, especially Koich, Patibo, and Payera, all largely Protestant areas, tended to predominate in educational employment. This was a further source of conflict.[52] The result was an intense rivalry between Protestant and Catholic throughout the district, and in the fifties a growing sense of discrimination on the part of the latter. Two Catholic papers published in the north by the Gulu Verona Fathers mission gave a good deal of attention to the alleged discrimination. In particular *Lobo Mewa* was convinced that Catholics were not getting a fair share in the allocation of resources.[53]

Although the UNC members of the appointments committee insisted that their objections to Opwa were on grounds of merit and efficiency, the Protestant bias of the committee (of both officials as well as unofficials) made it impossible to prevent allegations of religious discrimination. The situation was not made easier by the committee's dismissal, against the wishes of the District Commissioner, of three other African local government staff. It was out of this situation that inter-party politics developed. The early activities of the DP in Acholi district were specifically directed at challenging what they regarded as discrimination against the Catholic section of the community. Thus the second party emerged and the basis of inter-party politics at district level was established.

The DP established a branch in Acholi district after a visit by the Kampala leaders in 1956.[54] With its formation a number of Catholics who had originally been UNC supporters moved to the new party. The DP supporters who began to appear in the local councils were Catholics and the party was readily linked in the public and official mind with the Catholic Church.[55] In its early days the branch lacked any real party machine and party organization itself was minimal until 1958. Catholic Action contributed a good deal to bringing Catholics together. In addition the Verona Fathers mission, particularly at Kalongo in East Acholi, as has already been mentioned, were reported to be actively involved in politics, especially in persuading people to register for the elections in 1958.[56]

Then, however, in 1957 and 1958 local party leaders also began actively to seek to build up local support, using tactics very similar to those of the UNC. They set out to articulate local grievances, at grass roots level, moving among the rural population soliciting support. Their first local organizer, H. Obonyo (later to be one of the Acholi DP Members of the National Assembly) a teacher, recruited in 1957, gave up school holidays to cycling around Anaka, where he was then teaching, to establish local groups and appoint local officials. By 1960 teachers had become the party's main organizers. (Both parties in fact had by that stage considerable support from teachers.) The dominant local leader was however T. Okeny from East Acholi, who had previously worked in the Labour Department. He unsuccessfully contested the 1958 election as an independent but won a place on the district council. Okeny and Obonyo more than anyone else organized the party at the local level to win the 1959 district council election (the first direct elections for that body) albeit by a small majority. Okeny became council chairman.

The 1959 victory indicated the DP's ability to compete successfully with the UNC at grass roots level as they could not in Lango. But the DP's general platform did not differ markedly from that of the UNC so far as local grievances were concerned. The most significant difference between the two situations in terms of the polarization of political support around the two parties concerned the deeply felt religious rivalry in Acholi between Protestant and Catholic. Their prime concern with alleged religious discrimination was however one to which most Catholics responded. Consequently DP support was based largely on Catholic fears of discrimination at district level, especially in terms of educational services and posts in local government. The conflict over staff appointments pointed the way. The UNC leadership was predominantly Protestant; as a result their campaign against Opwa was interpreted in terms of religious discrimination. In addition some local UNC leaders undoubtedly spoke in highly critical and colourful language about the church generally and aroused additional fears of anti-religious action generally.[57] The Verona Fathers mission also actively campaigned for DP support among their parishioners, and against Protestant and UNC influence, building on existing local religious divisions. The involvement of teachers in party organization of both parties further drew the church into the battle.[58] This competition, sharpened by the existing inter-denominational friction in the district, aroused a deeply felt bitter political rivalry which became characteristic of Acholi politics. Party politics in Acholi, therefore, settled down along fundamentally religious lines, based upon long-established religious divisions. Neither party could establish real dominance. The close balance between them was demonstrated first in the 1958 election, when Opwa as DP candidate (who had lost much of any earlier popularity he had enjoyed) was defeated by Oola (UNC) by only 320 votes in a poll of 32,953. It was demonstrated for a second time by the close elections for the district council in 1959, and again by the close contests in the national elections of 1961 and 1962.

Thus two political parties each with genuine support emerged in the district. Both were represented in the district council which in 1959 therefore became a party council and thus a party forum. The existence of two parties meant that neither could afford to ignore any issue, particularly a local issue, that the other might exploit. In addition, at that time, 1958-59, when party support was being actively sought at grass roots level, the major resources parties would wish to control were concentrated at the district level. Control of the district council was thus of great importance for the district leadership. Neither party branch had close ties with its Kampala national headquarters and they developed much as they wished, with considerable autonomy. When in 1961 and 1962 the two national parties came to campaign for the general elections, it was on these autonomous branches that they were dependent for their support. The district leadership had established the mass support on which the heavy polls were based. But the district leaders had also established for themselves a position which frequently made them able to ignore national leaders' directions. Neither the UPC nor the DP national leadership was therefore able in 1961 and 1962 fully to control its own district leadership. UPC supported the East Acholi issue regardless of central policy; neither Obonyo nor Alexander Latim, both at the time ministers in the DP government could in 1961 control the DP in the district council over the *laloyo* issue.

The *laloyo* issue revived the earlier demands for a paramount chief for Acholi. The county chiefs, it will be remembered, had failed to win their campaign for a paramount in the late 1940s, although the post of *lawirwodi* that had been established was one of considerable influence. Acholi did not establish the post of elected unofficial chairman in 1956, when Lango separated the two offices. The *lawirwodi* remained therefore, in the late fifties, both chairman and chief executive of the district administration. The county chiefs controlled the office, since it had to be filled from among their numbers through election by the district council over which they still had considerable influence. The battle for political control of the district consequently included debate about this office.

By 1958 the Protectorate government was itself anxious to separate the two positions of council chairman and executive head of the district administration. This introduced a new phase in the struggle over district council organization, since by that time the unofficials, including the UNC, wanted a political district head with real executive power. Thus a battle very similar to that which took place in Lango developed. The provincial administration and the Ministry of Local Government favoured a permanent chief executive officer, a civil servant appointed by the appointments board, and a separate post of elected chairman, who might be a politician. The district council wanted an elected chief executive, also to be head of the district, whom they titled *laloyo*.[59] The renewed demand for such a leader was in 1958 strong influenced by Acholi reactions to the national scene and the feeling that they must have a leader who could meet the Kabaka, the Western Rulers, and the Kyabazinga on an equal footing. The growing intransigence of Buganda distinctly strengthened this feeling. The provincial administration however, whatever its views on the need for administrative reforms, was adamant against a political executive. Deadlock therefore ensued in the district council. After a good deal of argument the Ministry offered the council a choice: the chairman should be *laloyo*, a ceremonial head with no executive functions; the chairman should be elected, but the *laloyo*, the chief executive officer, should be appointed by the appointments board; there could be an office of laloyo-chairman; or finally there could be three offices: a *laloyo* (who would be a constitutional head), a chief executive, and a chairman. The council finally agreed (as did Lango) on a ceremonial head. New regulations in August

1959 abolished the post of *lawirwodi*, established a secretary, a senior executive officer, and an elected chairman of the council.[60]

Neither the DP nor the UNC leadership was convinced of the practicability of the idea of a *laloyo* but neither felt able to oppose an idea for which there appeared to be a good deal of popular support. Each party therefore wished to control the office.[61] Both had, however, to take into account the strong rivalries between the chiefdoms in the district, which affected distribution of political office, and could affect political support. The *laloyo* issue was essentially the latest phase in the contest for paramountcy between the major chiefdoms of Payera and Padibe.[62] The UNC had championed the return to the appointment of traditional chiefs in 1955. Whether or not they were genuinely committed to such an idea, their argument to the administration had been an appeal to traditional sentiment.

In the past the people were ruled by those members of the chieftainship and they were the people who used to choose such rulers after which they were to celebrate their royal appointments. . . The Acholi are very sad for the Uganda Government has abolished their system of appointing rulers. The Government is not appointing the real members of the chieftainship.

They had gone further to support the claim for a

permanent ruler who will rule over us and over our grandsons and we would like chances to be given us to elect this year. When the Government first came here they found Rwot Awich's father Rwot Camo Labwor was ruling and the Government wrote in the book 'King of Shuli', which meant Kabaka of Acholi.[63]

The UNC had thus committed themselves in 1956 to the Payera claim to Acholi paramountcy. This was not necessarily surprising, in view of Oola's Payera connection and the need at that time to expand UNC support in West Acholi. Later, in 1961, the UPC candidates for the West Acholi seats, Oola and Ojera, both Payera men, again supported Payera claims, implicitly if not openly, and the retired county chief, Yona Odida, of Payera, was regarded as the UPC candidate. This commitment, however, created an internal conflict within the party branch, since it challenged the Padibe claims to paramountcy, which UPC leaders from East Acholi could not afford to ignore. It also created a further inter-party conflict, since the DP supported the Pajule claims (for Philip Adongo) which in turn gave them the possibility of additional East Acholi support.

Neither party wished a decision to be made on the laloyoship until it was sure its own candidate would succeed. The UPC thus successfully forced through the Council a decision that the *laloyo* should be elected from among the 'leading families' because they believed this would be to their advantage. The DP, with a majority in the council, subsequently pushed through the election of their own candidate, against the instructions of the central government (itself at that time, early in 1962, a DP government), but with the support of certain UPC councillors from the East. The issue was not finally resolved until after independence but it indicated the manner in which internal Acholi cleavages could influence contemporary party politics.[64] The *laloyo* issue therefore increased inter-party rivalry, not least because it raised the old chiefdom rivalries which no party could ignore in its search for support.

The existence of the district council with its considerable resources therefore stimulated strong competitive party politics between the groupings within the district which, in the fifties, competed for representation in and control of the council. Between 1961 and 1962, when the DP and the UPC competed for office in the central government, neither party could afford to ignore the district level. They could not, therefore, afford to ignore the intermediary district leadership whose assistance they needed to obtain power at the district level. Both parties, however, for the most part maintained a careful division of authority between the two levels of leadership: in the district and at the centre. Both sought to accommodate the two groupings at the different levels and to seek the necessary compromise within the party itself by leaving the district with a considerable degree of autonomy.

# 6

## CONCLUSION

The pattern of politics in Acholi and Lango in the 1950s suggests that although Ugandan political parties failed to establish country-wide organization and control in those years, at the district level popular nationalist sentiment emerged which provided the foundations for the rapid expansion of the parties between 1960 and 1962. In the two districts local party branches successfully challenged both Protectorate government and chiefs for recognition as the legitimate political leaders. They did so primarily within the framework of the local government system which provided the most readily available forum through which that challenge could be made. Control of local government institutions became additionally important because they provided valuable political resources at the district level at a time when such resources scarcely existed at the centre. The party at district level, as it thus developed, was characteristically a small local leadership group but there was a basic popular sympathy which later provided the source of mass support.

Party leaders established their legitimacy at the district level largely by usurping the role of the chiefs as the recognized spokesmen of the local people. This was necessary for three reasons. First, the chiefs had in the past been regarded as the leaders of the people and the new political leaders had to transfer this role to themselves. Second, the chiefs represented governmental authority. Control over them therefore symbolized control over at least part of that authority. Gaining control over the appointment and dismissal of chiefs therefore gave the new party leaders in the district councils an important victory over the provincial administration, representing the Protectorate government, and also signified the victory of political power from below, office being acquired through election by the people, not bestowed from above. Third, chiefship carried with it status and reward and thus offered an important political resource. For all these reasons the district political leaders objected bitterly to the resumption of control over staff appointments by the Protectorate government in 1958 and the composition and functions of the regional service commission and district appointment boards were the causes of deep wrangling at the time of independence. It is not without significance

that at no time did anyone propose the abolition of the office of
chief (as occurred in Tanganyika). The office had become an integral
part of the district administrative machine and the politicians wished
to control that office, not to abolish it.

To control the office of chief and of local government staff generally the party at district level had to dominate the district administration. District activities consequently gave a good deal of time to the
acquisition of office at district level, in the district council and then
the district administration. Party organization for this purpose was
throughout rudimentary, partly because of the limited organizational
capacity of local leaders and partly because the local council system
offered an alternative. Nevertheless, from 1956 onwards a significant
number of the men elected as councillors had party allegiance.

Few of the district leaders who emerged in the 1950s to become
councillors had the necessary qualifications to move to the centre
when elections for the National Assembly took place in the early
sixties. Furthermore, by that time a new group of younger and more
educated men whose objective was the centre had entered both
parties. It was these men who became the parliamentary representatives at the centre, and the party tended therefore to divide the leadership between district and national leaders.

That it is dangerous to generalize for Uganda as a whole from
these two northern districts emerges from a very brief consideration
of West Nile, the third Northern Province district, over the same
period.[1] West Nile was the poorest and most remote of the three
districts. The large labour force that regularly travelled to work in
Buganda ensured that there was a good deal of information in the
district on other parts of the country, especially Buganda. Nevertheless the district remained the least politically active of the three.
Popular interest in the new local government structure introduced
in the late 1940s was slow to develop and it was not until the late
1950s that any such general interest showed itself.[2]

Within the district council itself there was a keen awareness of
local government developments elsewhere in the province, as was
shown in the resolution passed in 1952 requesting a constitution like
that of Acholi and Lango with an elected head of African local government and a principal judge.[3] These changes were introduced in 1953,
with the creation of the posts of *rwot madit* and chief judge, elected
by the district council from among the county chiefs.[4] West Nile also
followed the pattern laid down elsewhere when it adopted the 1955
District Councils Ordinance, and established the office of *agofe-obimo*,
chairman of the council and executive head of the district administration, elected by the council from among the county chiefs.[5] Senior

officials of the district administration therefore enjoyed a good deal of power. Direct elections for a substantial number of representative members were introduced in Madi sub-district council in 1956[6] and West Nile district council held direct elections by secret ballot in 1959.[7]

During the 1950s there was however little evidence of political party activity even in the 1959 elections. A UNC branch was set up in Arua in 1956 but it showed few signs of activity outside the town itself.[8] Although an occasional rally in Arua or at Packwach was reported in 1957 there had up to 1960 been few other signs of party activity, particularly in the lower level councils.[9] The Muslim population around Arua supported the branch but few people in the rural areas had any contact with it. There was very little evidence of local UNC leaders moving into the rural areas in these years.

Charles Onyutha, for example, who started the West Nile branch, left the district soon afterwards. When he returned he moved for a time into the splinter group of UPC. Nicolasio Abanya, a Lugbara trader-farmer prominent in the West Nile African Traders Association, who was in the branch at an early date, did not, so far as can be seen, set up rural groups as Engur did in Lango or Oola in Acholi. Another future UPC MP, Alex Lobidra, stood as an Independent in the 1958 Legislative Council elections, then went abroad, and only later joined UPC. Thus there was no real core of leaders with contacts in the villages, such as existed in Acholi and Lango. The Arua branch had Muslim support but this was concentrated around Arua and would probably not have been well received in non-Muslim rural areas. The small UNC group in Arua had nothing to match the Catholic church organization that supported Gaspare Oda in the 1958 election. They did not use the lower level councils, or the district council on which there were no known UNC activists in these years.[10]

The 1958 Legislative Council election was won by Gaspare Oda, formerly secretary of the West Nile district council who had represented the district in the Council since 1953. Although he stood as a DP candidate his victory was due not to party activity but to his own personal standing in the community and to the extensive support of the Catholics in a district where that church occupied a dominant position.[11] The DP had at that time established no more of a party machine in West Nile than had the UNC; nevertheless the religious divisions within the district, and the fact that 47 per cent of the population were Catholics,[12] gave them considerable support. Organizational church support made up for the absence of party machinery.

There were undoubtedly a number of factors that contributed to the slower development of party politics at the grass roots level

in West Nile than in Acholi and Lango. Official reports attributed
the problem to geographical isolation.[13] Equally important may have
been the ethnic complexity of the district and the division between
Lugbara and Alur.[14] It is not possible to enter into a detailed analysis
of these factors at this point. What does appear to be clear, however,
is that West Nile at that time lacked articulate 'new style' local
leaders, and much of the failure to establish party activity at grass
roots level in the 1950s was due to the absence of such leadership.
What UNC activity took place before 1960 suggested, for example,
an approach to political development very similar to that in Acholi
and Lango, based on attempts to associate local demands with national
issues. But the local leadership was unable to establish any firm base
over the district, outside Arua and its environs. Party politics did not
begin in West Nile until 1960, when a 'pronounced acceleration in the
pace at which party politics captured the imagination' was reported.[15]
Both major parties, concerned to organize on a country-wide basis for
the forthcoming general elections, gave a good deal of attention to
the district, and national leaders devoted much effort to establishing
branches and building up district leadership. New men thus came to
assist the party, although the earlier leadership was retained.[16] Moreover both parties campaigned on a combination of local and national
issues and both sought to gain control of district institutions as well
as national representation. Thus the West Nile district council elections of August 1961 (which followed close on the first general
election) were intensely contested on a purely party basis. Control of
local government was therefore important for party control at the
district level, even in a district which had been one of the last areas into
which the parties penetrated. In addition, the former branch leadership,
including UNC officials like Abanya, assumed the district leadership,
while the new men went as national representatives in the Legislative
Council and subsequently the National Assembly. The branch leadership was thus accommodated within district institutions.

A comparison between West Nile, Acholi and Lango in the 1950s
suggests therefore that the development of party political activity
was related to geography, the presence of a local leadership capable
of articulating existing grievances for their own purposes, and their
ability to establish some kind of network of communication across
the district. Notwithstanding the different period at which party
activity became significant, in all three instances attention was directed strongly at district institutions. An analysis of events elsewhere in Uganda over this period suggests a similar emphasis upon
district institutions.[17] This ought not to be surprising. The development of the local government system was common to the whole

country outside Buganda. Thus in each district there was the same good reason for seeking power at the local level and for local interests to compete for representation in and control of local government councils. The local government was a potential source of power in the district, distinct from, on the one hand, the provincial administration and, on the other, central government departments. Politically ambitious leaders therefore fought for control of that third force. In Ankole this brought a commoner, or *muiru*, to the post of *enganzi* by 1956, whereas it had previously been held by a member of the ruling *bahima* class.[18] In Bunyoro the emphasis upon local government led to a successful movement to turn the *omukama* into a constitutional ruler in his kingdom and to transfer power to an elected *rukurato*.[19] In Teso, on the other hand, rivalry at district level led to a conflict over local office so intense that by 1958 district administration was brought almost to a standstill and the Protectorate government felt bound to intervene.[20] Generally, therefore, the official emphasis upon local government institutions at district level encouraged political groups, including the parties, to seek power at that level. The democratization of the council was in all cases an important contributory factor to the growth of a new district political leadership and to the emergence of support in the rural areas for the parties to which that leadership belonged. UPC strength, particularly in the northern and eastern districts, was a legacy bequeathed it by the UNC, built up by active party groups at district level in the 1950s. Both major political parties, however, owed much of the mass support expressed in the elections of 1961 and 1962 to the earlier activities of local leaders within relatively autonomous districts. Thus the control of local government institutions was generally critical for party politics, particularly in the period 1960-1964, when competitive party politics was at its height.

A direct consequence of the emphasis upon local government and the creation of a district leadership was the extent to which national party leaders, when after 1960 they set out to establish their position in the country as a whole, had to acknowledge the district as the basic party unit and the importance of district leadership. They were obliged to support a number of district issues, such as East Acholi separation, or the creation of constitutional heads, which they might otherwise have ignored. Thus both parties between 1960 and 1962 supported a degree of district autonomy that conflicted with national policies for strong centralized control.

A further consequence was the implication that this district emphasis had for the growth of regional identity and a sense of corporate 'northern' activity. Early in the 1950s there was a general feeling that

Buganda had had too much preferential treatment, and that 'the north' was being left behind. In the mid-1950s, and more strongly after 1955 and the proposed constitutional changes of that year, there was a sense of the north as neglected. 'It is inevitable,' the Provincial Commissioner remarked, 'that the peoples of the Northern Province should look with envy at the greater density and numbers of secondary schools in the south; and that they should fear their districts are being left behind, a fear which is perhaps strengthened by the pace of political progress'.[21] Certainly there were expressions of antipathy towards Buganda and its dominant position.

Charles Onyutha, who stood as UPC candidate in 1958 in West Nile, challenged in his election manifesto the idea that the Kabaka should be King of Uganda. Oda, the DP candidate, wrote in his: 'Uganda's future self-determination will have to be granted as to one single country. In order to achieve this aim Government will be pressed upon to develop this country as one unity in social, economic and political fields without preferential treatment to any one particular vocal Province or district. . . .'[22] The UNC branch wrote to the Lukiko, in June 1958, that 'Self Government is Not for Buganda Alone'.[23] West Nile apprehensions were greatly increased at the time of the 1958 disturbances in Buganda, in which a number of Alur were killed. There were similar apprehensions in the other districts, and clear indications of 'jealousy and dislike of Buganda', comparable to that expressed in other parts of the country during these years.[24] Lango summed up the general feeling in a resolution in the district council in June 1958 against self-government under Buganda.

We fear that what Mengo Lukiko are doing, they want to spoil the relationships among the people of the Uganda Protectorate. They are opening a wide gap of hatred among the tribes. We and the other people in Uganda deplore the decision and maintain that we are not all in the group of people who bring about unwise decision.

We implore all Uganda Africans to have co-operation and unity among themselves. We implore them to progress in accordance with the wishes of the people of Uganda. Hatred among tribes in Uganda must now cease. In likewise we shall maintain the wish to achieve a unitary state of self-government which shall not compel us to be under any hereditary ruler whether we like it or not.[25]

As Buganda increasingly isolated itself from the rest of the country there was a corresponding hardening of attitudes against the kingdom and the concept of a 'state within a state'. The feeling was expressed in the Northern Province as elsewhere, by the district councils, by the UNC branches where they were articulate, and by the Members of the Legislative Council, all demanding equal treatment for their separate districts.

This fear of subordination to Buganda provided a common bond between the districts but it did not produce any movement to build up the province as a political balance to Buganda. There was in fact a clear awareness among some of the younger men of the danger of possible fragmentation that lay behind the principle of provincial autonomy.[26] Thus they rejected any idea of the separation of the Northern Province when they thought this was implied by Protectorate government actions. At the time of the Legislative Council debate on the 1955 District Councils Ordinance, for example, the Lango UNC sent a telegram to Fenner Brockway which emphatically rejected[27] 'any separation' from the rest of Uganda. A telegram from the Acholi UNC expressed the same fear, 'Acholi Congress passed resolution that Northern Province is and prefers to remain in Uganda Protectorate, protests against any separation from Uganda. . .'[28] The sense of neglect and the opposition to Ganda dominance did not therefore produce any marked sense of corporate provincial identity. The reaction was on the contrary towards a greater emphasis upon each individual district; an emphasis strengthened by inter-district rivalries and conflicts, such as the border disputes between Acholi and Lango. The chiefly leadership of the 1940s demanded 'native status' for each district, not for the province.[29] The new district party men took up this demand, in a somewhat amended form. These men, in the mid-1950s, accepted the general idea that it was necessary to endow the head of each district with real executive power, so that he would be treated by the government and the heads of other districts on an equal footing with the Bakama and the Kyabazinga.

The weakness of any sense of corporate provincial identity was demonstrated by the failure of successive official attempts to establish provincial level institutions. The Annual Report for the newly reinstated Northern Province had in 1947 noted a meeting of representatives from each district council to consider and make recommendations on matters of common interest. 'The meeting', it was reported, 'was a success and was welcomed by all Districts; as a result it is proposed to establish at an early date a Provincial Council consisting of members, official and elected, from each District Council.' This accorded with Governor Sir John Hall's preferred policy of building up the provinces as a balance to Buganda. But the provincial councils established in 1950 did not prove viable and Sir Andrew Cohen, Hall's successor, abandoned them in 1953. The causes of the failure were not difficult to see. On the one hand the provincial councils had been given no powers, except that of electing a provincial representative to the Legislative Council. On the other the districts were already jealous of their independent position. Busoga, for example, refused from the outset to participate in the Eastern Provincial Council which was consequently never gazetted.[30] The first attempt to create regional bodies thus failed.

In 1954, however, the Dreschfield Committee found Northern Province district councillors interested in the resuscitation of a Northern Province council. As a result, provision for advisory councils at provincial level was included in the 1955 Ordinance. In 1956 a Northern Province local government advisory council was consequently set up, with five representatives each from Acholi, Lango, and West Nile councils; two each from Madi sub-district and Karamoja; the chairmen of the Acholi, Lango, and West Nile councils; the Legislative Council representatives from each district; the *rwot adwong* of Lango; and the treasurers of Acholi, Lango, and West Nile. The Provincial Commissioner was chairman. The council would discuss matters of common interest to the local governments of the Northern Province and advise the Provincial Commissioner, when requested to do so, on local government matters.

This council met seven times, at irregular intervals, over the following three years. It did not however emerge as a significant institution.[31] Members did jointly discuss district political developments, such as the introduction of direct elections, or the separation of the posts of council chairman and chief executive officer, but the decisions were left for each district to take independently. No member suggested the council might be given greater powers.[32]

As events in Buganda in 1957 and 1958 made Northern district leaders more anxious about the future, they emphasized not the province but the district as their base and fought for increased powers at that level. But they also, especially the Legislative Council members, turned to the creation of more viable national political parties. Thus the answer to Buganda's intransigence was not a demand for increased powers for a Northern Province council or any other, but the decision, finally, in March 1960, to form the UPC. Once direct elections for the country as a whole had been decided on, the focus shifted even more rapidly from the province to the district and to the parliamentary constituency, within a unitary state. The rejection of provincial institutions was thus twofold: from district leaders who had won too much at that level to give it up; and from national leaders whose focus of attention was the national legislature and government. There was no *common* provincial front: no common delegations from the North, but rather from each district, to the successive enquiries of

the late 1950s. People might write to the papers as 'Northerners'.[33]
They fought elections as representatives of a district, and then of a
party, carrying with them to their parties the support built up in the
manner described in this essay.

# NOTE ON SOURCES

## (1) *Primary Sources*

District Records in Uganda Archives (Entebbe) and at District Headquarters at Gulu, Lira, and Arua.

A good deal of material for this study was obtained from district records, located in the Uganda Archives at Entebbe and at district headquarters at Gulu, Lira, and Arua. Uganda still had, in the 1960s, a rich store of such materials which if preserved will remain invaluable for future historians of the colonial period. This note deals only with the materials on Northern Uganda districts but it was made clear by the Archives Survey carried out in 1962 under the chairmanship of Mrs Barbara Saben that similar materials existed in most other districts. The records in the three northern districts of Acholi, Lango, and West Nile cover the period from the establishment of the colonial administration. The materials in West Nile were much more limited than in Acholi and Lango but in those two districts there was a large store of district files dating back to the 1920s. These included Touring Reports, Council Minutes and Reports, general administrative reports, the unpublished Annual District Reports (which provided the basis for the published report produced at provincial level), and general correspondence. There were also, at the time of my work, some useful records in the local authorities, relevant to district political development, including correspondence between local party leaders and district officials, concerning meetings, petitions, complaints, etc.

It is perhaps useful to point out that in fact considerable information about the development of the council system at both district and lower levels can be obtained from published sources, especially District Annual Reports and the Proceedings of the Legislative Council. Much detail on the Dreschfield Committee of 1955, for example, can be found in the Legislative Council debates of 1953 and 1955 on the proposed District Administration Ordinance. Unfortunately the Dreschfield Report itself (it was a Report of the Legislative Council, presented to that Council) does not appear to have survived.

## (2) *Government Publications*

Uganda Protectorate. *Annual Reports* on the Kingdom of Buganda, Eastern Province, Western Province, and Northern Province (Entebbe, Government Printer, 1947-1960).

C. A. G. Wallis, *Report of an Inquiry into African Local Government in the Protectorate of Uganda* (Entebbe, Government Printer, 1953) (hereafter referred to as *Wallis Report*).
*Northern Uganda: A Report on Rail and Road Communications in the North and North West of the Uganda Protectorate* (Entebbe, Government Printer, 1956) (hereafter referred to as *Northern Communications*).
*Land Tenure Proposals* (Entebbe, Government Printer, 1955).
*Report of the Uganda Relationships Commission, 1961* (Entebbe, Government Printer, 1961) (hereafter referred to as *Munster Report*).
*Report of the Constitutional Committee, 1959* (Entebbe, Government Printer, 1959) (hereafter referred to as *Wild Committee*).
*Proceedings of the Legislation Council, 1945–1962.*
*Report of the Commission of Inquiry into the Management of the Teso District Council* (Entebbe, Government Printer, 1958).

## (3) *Legislation*

The African Local Government Ordinance, *Laws of Uganda* Ch 74.
The African Authority Ordinance, *Laws of Uganda* Ch 72.
District Councils (District Administrations) Ordinance, No 1 of 1955.
African Authority (Amendment) Ordinance 1955, No 2 of 1955.
The Local Administrations Ordinance 1962, No 23 of 1962 (as amended by Ordinance 43 of 1962, and Acts 5 of 1962; 18 of 1963; 23 of 1963; 85 of 1963).
Administrations (Western Kingdoms and Busoga) Act, No 18 of 1963.
Constitutional Heads (Elections) Act, 1963, No 66 of 1963.
The Local Administrations Act 1967, No 18 of 1967 (as amended by Acts 17 of 1968; 19 of 1968; 1 of 1969; 31 of 1969).

## (4) *Books, Articles and Unpublished Dissertations*

D. E. Apter, *The Political Kingdom in Uganda* (Oxford, 1961).
C. Bryant, *Some Problems of Public Administration in Uganda* (unpublished PhD dissertation, London, 1963).
F. Burke, *Local Government and Politics in Uganda* (Syracuse NY, 1964).
A. Cohen, *British Policy in Changing Africa* (London, 1959).
M. Doornbos, 'Kumanyana and Rwenzururu: Two Responses to Ethnic Inequality' in R. I. Rotberg and A. A. Mazrui, *Protest and Power in Black Africa* (Oxford, 1970).
J. H. Driberg, *The Lango* (London, 1913).
A. G. G. Gingyera-Pinchywa, 'The Missionary Press and the Development of Political Awareness in Uganda in the Decade 1952-62: a case study from Northern Uganda', paper prepared for the East African Academy, Makerere University College, 17-20 September 1969.
F. K. Girling, *The Acholi of Uganda* (London, 1960).
Lord Hailey, *Native Administration and Political Development in British Tropical Africa* Part I (London, 1944).

Elspeth Huxley, *The Sorcerer's Apprentice* (London, 1959).

J. D. Lawrence, *The Iteso* (Oxford, 1957).

C. T. Leys, *Politicians and Policies: an Essay in Politics in Acholi 1962-1965* (Nairobi, 1967).

J. Lonsdale, 'Some Origins of Nationalism in East Africa', *Journal of African History*, vol ix, no 1 (1968).

D. A. Low, *Political Parties in Uganda 1945-1962* (London, 1962).

D. A. Low and C. Pratt, *Buganda and British Overrule* (Oxford, 1962).

M. Lowenkopf, *Political Parties in Uganda and Tanganyika* (unpublished MA dissertation, London, 1957).

A. Richards, *East African Chiefs* (London, 1960).

D. Rothchild and M. Rogin, 'Uganda', in G. Carter (ed.), *National Unity and Regionalism in Eight African States* (New York and London, 1966).

A. W. Southall, *Alur Society* (Cambridge, 1956).

A. W. Southall, 'Micropolitics in Uganda' (mimeo). Paper read at the conference of the East African Institute of Social and Economic Research, Kampala, 1963.

J. Stonehouse, *Prohibited Immigrant* (London, 1960).

H. R. Wallis, *Handbook of Uganda* (London, 1920).

'The Life of Yakobo Adoko as told to J. C. Huddle', *Uganda Journal*, vol xxi, no 2 (September 1957).

## (5) *Newspapers*

*Uganda Argus*

# NOTES

## PREFACE

1. See, for example, the special issue of the *Canadian Journal of African Studies*, vol iii, no 1 (Winter 1969) devoted to micropolitics in rural Africa.
2. Lonsdale, op. cit.
3. Southall, op. cit.
4. L. A. Fallers, *Bantu Bureaucracy* (Cambridge, 1956).
5. Leys, op. cit.
6. The most important sources on Buganda are Apter, op. cit., D. A. Low and L. A. Fallers (eds.), *The King's Men* (Oxford, 1964). A useful survey of Uganda is Rothchild and Rogin, op. cit.
7. See note on sources, pp.86-8.

## (1) INTRODUCTION

1. Uganda Census 1959, African Population, p.17. The 1969 figures were Buganda 2,667,332; Eastern 2,817,066; Western 2,432,550; Northern 1,631,899. (*Report on the 1969 Population Census*, vol 1 (Entebbe, Statistics Division, Ministry of Planning and Economic Development, 1971).)
2. See Low, op. cit. Also *Wild Committee*, paras. 1943-50.
3. Ibid., para. 65.
4. See J. S. Coleman and C. G. Rosberg, *Political Parties and National Integration in Tropical Africa* (Berkeley, 1964) or C. G. Haines, *Africa Today* (Baltimore, 1955).
5. Hailey, op. cit., ch. v Uganda, p.199.
6. *Munster Report*.
7. *Wild Committee*.
8. See C. Gertzel, 'Victory for the Kabaka', *Africa Report* (1962) also 'How Kabaka Yekka Came to be', *Africa Report* (October 1964).
9. *Munster Report*, para. 65.
10. The phrase was originally Milton Obote's.
11. Ali Mazrui has recently argued that Buganda's position constituted an important element in the integrative process in the 1950s, because it forced other Ugandans to concentrate on the question of power at the centre. This is not necessarily in conflict with the idea here that in order to contest for power at the centre non-Ganda leaders had, as I have suggested, to keep local issues in mind to ensure local support. See A. A. Mazrui, 'Privilege and Protest as Integrative Factors: The Case of Buganda's Status in Uganda', in R. I. Rotberg and A. A. Mazrui (eds.), *Protest and Power in Black Africa* (Oxford, 1970).
12. *A Report on the General Elections to the Legislative Council of the Uganda Protectorate held in March 1961* (Government Printer, Entebbe, 1961).

13. *A Report on the General Elections to the National Assembly of Uganda held on 25 April 1962* (Government Printer, Entebbe, 1962).

14. Cmnd 1778, *Uganda Independence Conference 1962.* See also H. F. Morris and J. S. Read, *Uganda*, vol 13, *The British Commonwealth: The Development of its Laws and Constitutions* (London, 1966) pp.78–9.

15. The Local Administrations Ordinance, 1962, No 23 of 1962, s.21.

16. Especially Acts 5 of 1962 and 85 of 1963, which increased the Minister for Regional Administration's authority to intervene in financial matters and made appointments of secretary-general and financial secretary subject to his confirmation.

17. Act No 18 of 1967, The Local Administrations Act, 1967.

## (2) NORTHERN UGANDA

1. Hailey, op. cit., p. 192. The District population figures in the 1948 Census were Lango 265,890; Acholi 215,655; West Nile and Madi 336,063; Karamoja 125,567.

2. *Annual Report*, Northern Province, 1949.

3. *Northern Communications*, p.31. The Report contains a detailed study of the northern economy in 1954. Climatic conditions contributed greatly to the 1953 adverse figures.

4. *District Report, Lango*, 1950 (unpublished).

5. Southall, op. cit., ch x.

6. *Annual Report*, Northern Province, 1956.

7. *Northern Communications*, p.37.

8. There is still considerable movement between South Lango and Bulemezi county of Bunyoro across the lake. Traditionally Lake Kyoga has been not a barrier but a trade route, but trade with Bunyoro seems to have collapsed, presumably with the collapse of Bunyoro at the end of the nineteenth century. For this point and other information on Lango's commercial relations with Bunyoro I am grateful to Dr Louise Pirouet, formerly of Makerere University, Kampala.

9. A. Richards (ed.), *Economic Development and Tribal Change* (Cambridge, 1954) especially chs. III and IV. See also *Northern Communications*. Ganda farmers employed a good deal of migrant labour on their farms.

10. Lango District Archives, ADM 9/5. Touring Report for Dokolo County, Assistant District Commissioner to District Commissioner, 4 October 1948.

11. *African Education in Uganda* (De Bunsen Report) (Entebbe, Government Printer 1953).

12. E. P. A. Schleh, 'The Post War Careers of Ex-Servicemen in Ghana and Uganda', *Journal of Modern African Studies*, vol vi, no 2 (1968).

13. Entebbe Secretariat Archives, ADM 21(L) Letter from Lango in Nairobi to Lango Native Council, 18 May 1946.

14. This became more so when the Protectorate government proposed changes in land tenure in 1955. See below, pp.39–40.

15. E.g., *District Report, Lango*, 1949 (unpublished) p.57.

16. Ibid. See also Girling, op. cit., p.185.

17. Stonehouse, op. cit.

18. T. Hodgkin, *Nationalism in Colonial Africa* (London, 1956). See also J. Saul in G. Ionescu and E. Gellner (eds.), *Populism* (London, 1969), and Lonsdale, op. cit.

19. Coleman, op. cit., passim.

## (3) THE EVOLUTION OF LOCAL ADMINISTRATION

1. For a survey of the Uganda Administration see generally Hailey, op. cit.

2. There is some disagreement as to how much direct supervision was placed over chiefs in Buganda. See Low and Pratt, op. cit., especially ch. 11. Also Fallers, op. cit. Chiefs had to report regularly to administrative offices in Buganda. Nevertheless the absence of a ruler such as the Kabaka and ministers of the status of the Kabaka's ministers in the non-agreement districts meant immediately a more direct control. In the western kingdoms the position stood somewhere in between.

3. Acholi Local Government Estimates 1954-1955.

4. On the position, power, and functions of chiefs in the 1950s see especially Richards, op. cit.

5. Hailey, op. cit., is useful for basic comparisons on the development of the council system in Uganda. See also Ministry of Regional Administration (hereafter MRA) LGI 6541. Native Councils (1930), also Entebbe Archives, C.175. Native Administration, General Policy, Eastern Province (1941).

6. Ibid. Also Lawrence, op. cit., p.39.

7. C.175. Native Administration, General Policy, Eastern Province (1941).

8. Lord Hailey, *Native Administration and Political Development in the British Colonial Territories* (London, 1950), has a useful summary of the position in 1950. See also MRA 1948, Constitutions of Councils in all Provinces. (Governor Sir Philip Mitchell's ideas about the reform necessary in the administrative structure must also have been of considerable importance in these developments. See his *Native Administration* (Government Printer, Entebbe, 1939) for official use only.) For a description of this council system in action in 1949 see Huxley, op. cit., pp. 199-200, and for an account of the proceedings in one sub-county council in Busoga in 1950 and 1951 see Fallers, op. cit., App. IV.

9. *Laws of Uganda*, ch. 74, 'An Ordinance to define the Composition of African Local Governments and to make Provisions for the Reconstitution of African Councils through the Protectorate'. These posts had already been introduced administratively in some districts, starting in Teso in 1942.

10. Despatch from the Secretary of State for the Colonies to the Governors of the African Territories, 25 February 1947. See Bryant, op. cit., especially ch. 5.

11. *Wallis Report*, Part I.

12. *Uganda Legislative Council Proceedings*, 12 January 1955, Debate on the Second Reading of the Bill.

13. *Laws of Uganda*, Ch. 72.

14. *Report of the Commission of Inquiry into the Management of the Teso District Council*, March 1958 (Entebbe, Government Printer, 1958).

15. *Uganda Legislative Council Proceedings*, 5 May 1958, Second Reading of District Administration (District Councils) (Amendment) Bill 1958.

16. *Wallis Report* paras. 12 and 13.

17. There is a very full discussion of this Committee in *Uganda Legislative Council Proceedings*, 12 January 1955, in the debate on the Second Reading of the Bill. See also the debates on 23 November 1953 and 13 April 1954. There are reports of the meetings held with this Committee (hereafter called the Dreschfield Committee) in the districts in a number of district archives.

18. Low, op. cit., p.15.

19. Acholi District Archives. J. W. Steil, *Notes on Native Administration and Political Development in Northern Province*, June 1947.

## (4) POLITICS IN LANGO DISTRICT 1945–1962

1. Hailey (1950), p.61. See Driberg, op. cit., for Lango organization. No anthropological study of the Lango has been done since Driberg's original work except T. Hayley, *The Anatomy of Lango Religion and Groups* (Cambridge, 1947). Information on tribal structure and customs is found in works on the Nilotic peoples generally.

2. Much of the biographical information involved in the Lango scene in this period was obtained from interviews with the men concerned, who were generous in the time they gave to discuss the district's history with me. Annual District Reports also contained information about staff.

3. Lango District Archives, ADM 20. Chiefs and Members of the Lango Council to the Governor, 12 December 1944.

4. Hailey (1944), op. cit. Also Lawrence, op. cit., p 38.

5. A post for which he soon proved unsuitable. He was moved to the post of native administration secretary. He then became district representative in the Legislative Council, from 1953 to 1957.

6. The *won nyaci* campaign can be followed in Lira District Archives, *Lango District Annual Reports* (unpublished). Also C183/3 Provincial Commissioner to Secretary for African Affairs 30 January 1947.

7. In 1919 the Protectorate government had agreed to the appointment of a permanent president of the Busoga District Council, with the title of Kyabazinga. In the 1940s the Busoga Council was seeking to establish this as an hereditary office. See Fallers, op. cit.

8. See, for example, Lango District Archives, ADM 20, Lango Native Council Minutes, Voting for *won nyaci*, in letter from five county chiefs to District Commissioner, 27 June 1945.

9. Hailey (1944), op. cit., mentions the Young Lango Association challenge to the chiefs. See Lango District Archives, ADM/20/2, Young Lango Association.

10. Lango District Archives, *District Report*, Lango, 1948 (unpublished).

11. Entebbe Secretariat Archives, Secretary for Native Affairs to Provincial Commissioner, Northern Province, 13 September 1950; Provincial Commissioner to Secretary for Native Affairs, 19 September 1950. Also see Legal Notices 54 and 55 of 1951.

12. Lango District Archives, *District Report*, Lango, 1947 (unpublished).

13. Hailey (1950), op. cit., p.64, says ten peasants, but District records gave twenty.

14. Lango District Archives, Memo on Native Administration 1947. See also the *District Reports* for 1944–1947.

15. Lango District Archives, Standing Orders, in Lango District Council *Minutes* for October 1946.

16. When the 1949 Local Government Bill was debated in the Legislative Council Mr Ringe, from West Nile District, while welcoming the legislation on behalf of the peoples of the Northern Province, asked for an assurance that 'the present system [of appointment of chiefs] whereby Councils submit names for approval either by Higher Councils or by the District or Provincial Commissioner will not be altered'. He also expressed the hope that at some future date chiefs would be appointed by councils without reference to the Protectorate government. The Chief Secretary assured him there would be no change in the system of nomination and did not rule out the second possibility. See *Proceedings of Legislative Council*, 2 March 1949, p.119.

17. This is based on evidence of the Touring Reports for each county from

1945 onwards in the Lango District Archives. This kind of discussion was in fact exactly what the administration had hoped would develop. See Lango District Archives, ADM 975. Assistant District Commissioner to District Commissioner, 30 September 1947. The trouble was that some council members went further than a liberal but paternalistic administration believed politically desirable.

18. Entebbe Secretariat Archives, C183/3, Elected Members of Lango District Council to the Governor, 28 November 1951.

19. Entebbe Secretariat Archives, Provincial Commissioner, Northern Province, Note on the Administration in the Northern Province, 14 June 1947.

20. Lango District Archives, *Minutes* of the Lango Native Council, 20 May 1946.

21. Entebbe Secretariat Archives, District Commissioner, 14 December 1948.

22. It was the same in other districts. See Huxley, op. cit., p.199.

23. Lango District Archives. *Minutes* of Lango District Council, April 1950.

24. Entebbe Secretariat Archives C183/3. African Local Government, letter from Elected Members to Governor, 28 November 1951.

25. The district team consisted of all provincial administration and departmental officers, and included the senior African local government officials. It was charged with the co-ordination of district development activity.

26. 'Life of Yakobo Adoko . . .', op. cit.

27. *Proceedings of Uganda Legislative Council*, 12 January 1955. For this Committee also, see above, p.22.

28. *Sessional Paper No 4 of 1956-1957.*

29. Information on the origins of the UNC in Lango is derived primarily from interviews with the original party leaders, to whom I am most grateful for assistance. District Reports also contain information on the party, as do Lango Local Government Archives.

30. See Stonehouse, op. cit., p.66, on his visit to Lira in 1951. 'I stayed that night with Yokasofati Engur, the young leader of the farmers in Lango district . . . Engur himself is an intelligent, sincere man. We sat up half the night talking about Uganda's problems . . . Engur talked not only about political advance, he thought a great deal could be done in his own area by irrigation and cultural improvements . . .'

31. This became an issue when Sir Andrew Cohen proposed, as part of the introduction of a ministerial system in 1956, to appoint Mr (later Sir) Amar Maini, a prominent Kampala Asian, as a Minister in the Executive Council. In spite of strong opposition he did so and the agitation died down. Legislative Councillors, however, later successfully opposed the introduction of any specific Asian representation in the legislature.

32. Lango District Council Archives, M 15/5/8, Uganda National Congress, contains a record of all these meetings. See also Lango District Archives, CSW, UNC. Also *Annual District Reports*, passim.

33. *Lango District Annual Report 1955* (unpublished).

34. *Land Tenure Proposals* (Entebbe, Government Printer, 1955).

35. Lango District Archives, ADM 9/6. Kwania Reports. Kwania tour January-February 1956. Such feelings were expressed in a different way in 1959, when it was suggested that some Nandi should be settled in the district.

36. Lango District Council Archives, M 15/5/8, Report of meeting of 3 March 1956.

37. Ibid.

38. *Uganda Argus*, 6 November 1956. See also *Lango District Annual Report 1956* (unpublished).

39. *Lango District Annual Report* 1953 (unpublished).
40. Lango District Archives, Erute County Book 1953.
41. Ibid., 1953.
42. Ibid., Report of 1 June 1954.
43. Low, op. cit., passim.
44. Lango District Council Archives M 15/5/8.
45. The disposition of chiefs and unofficials in the district council in the early 1950s in relation to voting suggests that Engur and his UNC associates may have supported the claims of his uncle, Yakabo Adoko, to a senior position in the district, against those of Rwot Isaya Ogwangunjji and his half brother Rwot Eria Olet. Such an alliance between UNC and one faction among the county chiefs would explain Engur's ability to win a small majority vote in the council in 1956 (see below). Such family alliances cannot be ignored in the early UNC position.
46. *Minutes* of the Lango District Council, 1 February 1956. When Engur was subsequently jailed for his part in the land riots, he lost his seat in the council.
47. Ibid., 14-18 May 1957.
48. See above, p.44.
49. *Legal Notice 213 of 1959*.
50. These events can be followed in the *Minutes* of the Lango District Council which discussed the issue at length during 1960.
51. Local Administrations (Amendment) Act, June 1963. See above, p.7.
52. Engur, the *won nyaci*, B. Otim as secretary-general and S. G. Okelo-Olong as financial secretary. See *Uganda Argus* 12 July 1963. Engur subsequently became Uganda's Ambassador to Russia and Otim replaced him as *won nyaci*.
53. *A Report on the First Direct Elections to the Legislative Council of the Uganda Protectorate* (Government Printer, Entebbe, 1958). The other candidates were J. Okae, PP; S. Okelo-Olong, UPC; B. Olwit, DP.
54. Ibid. Each district was left free to choose whether or not it would elect its Legislative Councillors by direct or indirect elections. Internal political disagreements led the other districts to reject direct elections.
55. *Lango District Annual Reports* 1956 and 1957 (unpublished).
56. 'Road to the Top', biographical note on Obote in *Free Uganda* (Kampala, 1962).
57. *Uganda Herald*, 24 April 1952 and 28 October 1952. I am grateful for this reference to Mr Brian Bowles, University of Dar es Salaam.
58. Obote, by report, kept very quiet at such interviews but his presence was significant.
59. *Proceedings of the Uganda Legislative Council*, 12 March 1958.
60. *Minutes* of Lango District Council, 2 August 1958.
61. *Proceedings of the Uganda Legislative Council*, 5 May 1958.
62. Obote appears to have assumed the actual leadership of Lango UNC from the time he returned home in 1956; he did not however publicly take up this role until he moved into the Legislative Council in 1958.
63. Apter, op. cit.; Low, op. cit.
64. Ibid.
65. Lango District Archives, *Erute County Book*, 26 June 1957.
66. Lango District Archives, *Touring Reports*, passim.
67. *Lango District Annual Report*, 1958 (unpublished).
68. *Reports* of the 1961 and 1962 Elections, op. cit.
69. Rothchild and Rogin, op. cit., p.379. See above.
70. Ibid., p.380.

71. *Uganda Census 1959*, African Population, p.66.
72. Lango District Archives M/s 12/7, District Commissioner to I. Acanga, 11 July 1952.
73. Interview with Mr Acanga.
74. *Lango District Annual Report*, 1956 (unpublished).

## (5) PARTY POLITICS IN ACHOLI DISTRICT 1945–1962

1. For this background of the Acholi system I am indebted to Professor B· Webster, Professor of History at Makerere University, who provided me with information on the traditional political systems of Acholi and Lango collected in the course of the intensive researches he and his colleagues and students have undertaken into Uganda's pre-colonial history over the past four years. Generously he tried to eliminate my earlier mistakes and misunderstandings. Those which remain are my responsibility.
2. MRA, 1948. Constitutions of Councils of all Provinces. On the development of the Council system see Hailey (1944), op. cit., ch. 1, section v. British officials of the period, when referring to 'clan', almost certainly meant 'chiefdom'.
3. Entebbe Archives, C183/3. Acholi, African Local Government Ordinance, Memo by Provincial Commissioner, Northern Province, 1947.
4. E.g., Acholi District Archives, ADM 31/A. PCNP Gulu. Acholi District Council, Resolutions of Meeting, 8 October 1947.
5. See above p.17.
6. Acholi District Archives, *Acholi District Annual Report*, 1949 (unpublished).
7. Acholi District Archives, *Acholi District Annual Report*, 1950 (unpublished). Provincial Commissioner, 19 September 1950.
8. Entebbe Archives, ADM 21/A. Acholi District Council, *Minutes* of Meeting, 12 April 1949.
9. Acholi District Archives, *Acholi District Annual Report*, 1950 (unpublished). Legal Notice 54 of 1957, Acholi District Council (Amendment) Regulations, 1957.
10. Acholi District Archives, *Acholi District Annual Report*, 1957 (unpublished).
11. Much of the information on which the following account of the origins of the UNC in Acholi is based was obtained from interviews with people associated with the movement in its early days, among whom a strong tradition from that period has remained. Each UNC group in East Acholi, for example, in 1962 still retained a file of early letters and documents concerning the formation of the party and remembered vividly the circumstances of early party activity. Documentary evidence is also contained in *Touring Reports* in Acholi District Archives, then held (in 1962) in Gulu and Kitgum.
12. Acholi District Council Archives, SCW/8 District Commissioner to Y. Engur, 11 June 1953.
13. Acholi District Archives, Lamwo County Touring Reports, 3 May 1954.
14. Ibid., SCW/7. P. Oola to District Commissioner, May 1954.
15. Acholi Local Government Archives, L.G. 69/P & I. Assistant District Commissioner, Kitgum, to P. Oola, 17 November 1954.
16. Acholi District Archives, Lamwo Touring Reports, 24 November 1954.
17. The change in the method of election (under the new Regulations of 1956) by which the sub-county became an electoral college for the district council was to the advantage of the UNC, although it still left elections open to the influence of the chiefs.

18. Acholi District Archives, Notes on Acholi District 1959.

19. Acholi District Archives, Agago Touring Reports, 29 September 1961.

20. Acholi District Archives, C.ADM 9/6. Lamwo Tour Book, 3 January 1961.

21. Mr Lalobo, the Assistant Agricultural Officer, for example, obviously played an important intermediary role. He subsequently lost his pension rights because of alleged involvement with the UPC. The UPC/KY government restored them by Act No 4 of 1963.

22. Leys, op. cit., p.26.

23. Acholi District Council Archives, SCW/8.

24. Acholi District Archives, SCW/8. Acholi UNC to Provincial Commissioner, nd, but received 10 February 1955; ibid., UNC to District Commissioner, 23 June 1955.

25. Acholi District Council Archives, SCW/8. UNC/DC 23 June 1955.

26. Acholi District Archives, Lamwo Tour Book, 26 June 1956.

27. Acholi District Council Archives, SCW/8. DC to Oola, 16 August 1955. Oola's list of candidates was interesting, since it consisted of men who were not only UNC supporters but also in most cases men of more education than the existing branch leadership. Four of his seven candidates had been to Makerere.

28. Acholi District Archives, LG69, Part I, 1954, UNC.

29. Acholi District Council Archives SCW/8. P. Oola to DC, 22 April 1953.

30. Ibid., petition 28 August 1957.

31. Acholi District Archives, C.ADM.9/2. Agago Touring Reports, February 1958.

32. Ibid., Chua Report, January–February 1961.

33. Acholi District Archives, Meeting with Dreschfield Committee, July 1954.

34. Acholi District Archives, C.ADM 9/4. Touring Report, Obyen Division.

35. Acholi District Council Archives, SCW/8 Acholi UNC to PC, nd, but stamped 10 February 1955.

36. *Acholi District Annual Report*, 1956 (unpublished), p.133.

37. Interviews with local UNC officials and supporters.

38. Acholi District Archives, Chua Touring Reports, 5 January 1956. The Acholi District Council did not introduce direct elections until 1962.

39. Acholi District Archives, C.ADM 9/6. Lamwo Touring Book, ADC to DC 18 September 1956.

40. Memorandum for the Munster Commission prepared by the East Acholi Assembly, nd. I am grateful to Mr B. Okwok for a copy of this Memorandum.

41. Acholi District Archives, LG69, Part I.

42. Acholi District Archives, C.ADM 9/4. Touring Reports, ADC to DC, 21 August 1958, Chua Safari.

43. Acholi District Archives, *Acholi District Annual Report*, 1958 (unpublished).

44. See, e.g., Acholi District Council Archives, SCW 8/34, Kitgum files, Report of Fourth Meeting of Acholi District Council, 19 July 1959.

45. *Munster Report*, paras. 256–8.

46. Acholi District Council Archives, SCW 8/34. Kitgum. Minutes of East Acholi Assembly, 19 July 1959.

47. Memorandum to the Munster Commission, 1961. Also personal communication.

48. On all three occasions in 1959, 1961 and 1962, the question of East Acholi probably lost the UNC votes in the area.

49. Acholi District Council files, SCW/8. Acholi UNC to PC, 10 February 1955.

50. *Proceedings of the Legislative Council*, 12 January 1955.

51. *Uganda Argus*, 15 February 1956.

52. Acholi District Council Archives, SCW/8, UNC to DC, 21 August 1957. Also Acholi District Council Minutes, 1956-1958, passim.

53. Acholi District Archives, A2501. Petitions, Misc. Northern Province.

54. Girling, op. cit., p.187. *Acholi District Annual Report*, 1956 (unpublished). For statistics on religious affiliation see Uganda Census 1959, African Population, p.66.

55. See Gingyera-Pincywa, op. cit.

56. Acholi District Archives, *Acholi District Annual Report*, 1957 (unpublished).

57. Acholi District Archives, Agago Touring Reports, 4 February 1958; Chua Report, May 1957.

58. Ibid., 2 March 1958.

59. Acholi District Archives, C.ADM 9/2, ADC to DC, 4 February 1958, Kitgum.

60. Acholi District Archives, C.ADM 9/4, ADC to DC, September 1960.

61. Acholi District Archives, C.ADM 20/2. DC to Permanent Secretary, Ministry of Local Government, 13 June 1960. Also C.1453. Laloyo. Meeting of District Commissioners, NP, November 1957.

62. The battle was fought with considerable publicity in the district council and can be followed in the Council Minutes 1958-1963.

63. Acholi District Council Archives, SCW 8. Acholi UNC to PC, 10 February 1955. Rwot Awich, who had succeeded his father, Rwot Ochama, as head of Payera in 1887, had been a dominant personality in Acholi and was generally regarded as a paramount by Payera people. As a result the Payera clan had claimed an ascendancy over the whole of Acholi which was rejected by both East Acholi chiefdoms, especially Padibe, and the Protectorate government.

64. See Leys, op. cit., pp.19-21.


## (6) CONCLUSION

1. On West Nile see especially Southall, op. cit., particularly ch. x for a description of West Nile in the early 1950s. Also Southall, 'Micropolitics in Uganda' (mimeo), paper read at the Conference of the East African Institute of Social and Economic Research, Kampala, 1963. My brief note on West Nile is based on material in the district archives, which are much more scanty than those of Acholi or Lango, and interviews with local leaders. I am most grateful to Professor Southall for his assistance in giving me a greater understanding of West Nile. The conclusions suggested here are of course my own. Since I did my fieldwork other and more detailed research on West Nile has been carried out, especially by Dr A. G. G. Gingyera-Pincywa of Makerere Univeristy and Mrs Anne King of Sussex University.

2. Southall, op. cit.

3. West Nile District Archives, Notes on West Nile by Bere (PC) to Boyd (Entebbe), 23 July 1952.

4. West Nile District, *Annual Report* 1953 (unpublished).

5. West Nile District, *Annual Report* 1956 (unpublished). Legal Notice No 210 of 24 November 1955.

6. Northern Province, *Annual Report* 1956, p.129.

7. Northern Province, *Annual Report* 1959, p.94.

8. West Nile District Archives, SCW/UNC, contains local correspondence concerning party activists; see also ADM.9 Touring Reports.

9. Ibid. Also Southall, 'Micropolitics', op. cit.

10. West Nile District, *Annual Report* 1958 (unpublished). Also West Nile Archives, SCW, Election Petition to High Court by Charles Onyutha, in Onyutha to Godfrey Binaisa, 27 October 1958.

11. *Uganda Census 1959,* African Population, p.66.

12. Northern Province, *Annual Report* 1960, p.11.

13. See Southall, 'Micropolitics', op. cit.

14. Ibid. Also West Nile District Archives, SCW, UNC.

15. West Nile District, *Annual Report* 1960 (unpublished).

16. This does not mean that they had not earlier held positions in the district. Thus Felix Onama, for example, who became the dominant Madi UPC figure, built up a considerable base in the co-operative movement and as manager of the West Nile ginnery. He had not, however, before 1960, been active for the UNC at district level. He had originally been a member of the DP, moving to the UPC in 1961.

17. Secondary sources still remain inadequate for a full understanding of party growth over Uganda as a whole in the 1950s. Apter, op. cit., includes an account of early activity but no great detail. *Annual Reports* of each district contain some information. This section here is based on limited fieldwork in several other districts, official documentation for those districts, and discussions with leaders.

18. Doornbos, op. cit.

19. A. R. Dunbar, *A History of Bunyoro-Kitara* (Oxford, 1965), ch. 18. Also MRA Ad Hoc Touring Committee on District Councils Bill, Report of Public Meeting at Hoima, August 1954.

20. See above, pp.20–21. Also *Report on the Teso Administration 1958*, op. cit.

21. *Uganda Herald* 24 April 1952, for a letter from Milton Obote on this theme. I am grateful to Mr Bowles for this reference.

22. Northern Province *Annual Report* 1956. See also MRA, C 1025/1.

23. West Nile District Archives. Candidates' Manifestoes for 1958. Legislative Council Elections in West Nile

24. West Nile District Archives, SCW/UNC. UNC West Nile Branch to Lukiko of Buganda 15 June 1958.

25. Low, op. cit., p.29.

26. Lango District Council Minutes June 1958

27. *Proceedings of Legislative Council* November 1953.

28. Lango District Council Archives. LG 69 Part I. UNC to Fenner Brockway 10 January 1955.

29. Acholi District Council Archives. LG 69 Part I.

30. *Wallis Report*, para. 12.

31. Bryant, op. cit., p.198.

32. Acholi District Archives. *Minutes* of Northern Province Council 1957-1960.

33. *Uganda Argus* 28 June 1955. This reference was also kindly first pointed out to me by Mr Bowles.

# INDEX